COPING SKILLS FOR KIDS

HELP YOUR YOUNG CHILDREN THRIVE: A PARENTING GUIDE FOR DEVELOPING YOUR CHILD'S RESILIENCE, SELF-CONFIDENCE, AND EMOTIONAL INTELLIGENCE THROUGH 103 PLAYFUL AND ENGAGING GAMES

KIDS SLT PUBLICATIONS

Copyright Kids SLT Publications 2023 - All rights reserved.

The content contained within this book may not be reproduced, duplicated, or transmitted without direct written permission from the author or the publisher.

Under no circumstances will any blame or legal responsibility be held against the publisher, or author, for any damages, reparation, or monetary loss due to the information contained within this book. Either directly or indirectly. You are responsible for your own choices, actions, and results.

Legal Notice:

This book is copyright protected. This book is only for personal use. You cannot amend, distribute, sell, use, quote, or paraphrase any part, or the content within this book, without the consent of the author or publisher.

Disclaimer Notice:

Please note the information contained within this document is for educational and entertainment purposes only. All effort has been executed to present accurate, up to date, and reliable, complete information. No warranties of any kind are declared or implied. Readers acknowledge that the author is not engaging in the rendering of legal, financial, medical, or professional advice. The content within this book has been derived from various sources. Please consult a licensed professional before attempting any techniques outlined in this book.

By reading this document, the reader agrees that under no circumstances is the author responsible for any losses, direct or indirect, which are incurred as a result of the use of the information contained within this document, including, but not limited to, — errors, omissions, or inaccuracies.

CONTENTS

Introduction ... 9

1. EMOTIONAL INTELLIGENCE— WHAT'S THE BIG DEAL? ... 15
   What Is Emotional Intelligence ... 16
   The Benefits of EQ for Children ... 19
   Emotional Intelligence Can Be Learnt ... 20
   Your Child Is a Sponge ... 23
   Children Who May Have Extra Difficulties with Emotional Intelligence ... 25

2. EMOTIONAL DEVELOPMENT MILESTONES ... 27
   Defining Social and Emotional Development ... 28
   The 3 Major Emotional Stages in Childhood Development ... 29
   Emotional Milestones for Babies ... 33
   Emotional Milestones for Toddlerhood ... 35
   Emotional Milestones for Pre-schoolers ... 37
   Emotional Milestones for 5 to 6-Year-Olds ... 39
   How to Foster Emotional Development Throughout the Early Years ... 41

3. LISTENING TO YOUR CHILD ... 49
   What Is Active Listening ... 50
   How to Practice Active Listening With Your Child ... 51
   Children's Moods and Their Triggers ... 54
   Identifying Your Child's Triggers ... 55
   How to Help with Trigger Awareness ... 57
   8 Kid-Power Emotional Safety Techniques for All Ages ... 61

4. THE IMPORTANCE OF SETTING HEALTHY
   BOUNDARIES 67
   What Are Personal Boundaries 68
   Why Boundaries Matter 70
   Let's Double Check Your Boundaries Are In
   Place 72
   How to Teach Your Child About Boundaries ... 75
   Your Child Has the Right to Say No— Teach
   Them How! 80
   Games and Activities to Teach Boundaries ... 82

5. "TELL ME HOW YOU REALLY FEEL" 87
   Arts and Crafts 89
   Songs and Word Games 93
   Organising Emotions 96
   Ideas for Mindset 99
   Burning off Pent up Emotions 103
   Using Technology 106

6. LET'S TALK ABOUT BODY LANGUAGE ... 109
   What Is Body Language? 110
   Focus on the Facial Expressions 111
   What Your Child's Gestures Mean 113
   How Do People Use Body Language to
   Express Different Emotions? 115
   10 Things to Teach Your Child About Body
   Language 117
   Activities to Help With Body Language 120

7. HELPING YOUR CHILD COPE WITH BIG
   FEELINGS 127
   What Does Emotional Dysregulation Look
   Like? 128
   Understanding The Polyvagal Theory and 7
   Activities to Practice It 130
   What Parents Can Do to Help Children With
   Self-Regulation 136
   13 Mindful Exercises for Children 139

Coping Tips and Tricks for Warm to Hot
　　Emotions　　　　　　　　　　　　　　　　147
　　When to Seek Professional Help　　　　　150

8. YOU HAVE GOT THIS: 13 ACTIVITIES JUST
　　FOR PARENTS AND CAREGIVERS　　　153
　　Emotional Regulation Self-Assessment　　153
　　Self-Care　　　　　　　　　　　　　　　　154
　　Take Five—Religiously!　　　　　　　　　155
　　Take a Digital Detox　　　　　　　　　　155
　　Rewiring Negative Thoughts　　　　　　　156
　　Using Affirmations　　　　　　　　　　　157
　　How is Your Mindset?　　　　　　　　　　158
　　STOPP　　　　　　　　　　　　　　　　　158
　　How Big Are Your Problems?　　　　　　159
　　Reassess the People in Your Life　　　　　160
　　Understand the Power of Choice　　　　　160
　　Step Back From Perfectionism　　　　　　161
　　Have Fun　　　　　　　　　　　　　　　162

　　Conclusion　　　　　　　　　　　　　　163
　　References　　　　　　　　　　　　　　169

BONUS #1

Develop Early Skills

If your child has delayed Speech, Language and Communication skills then you need this bonus! Use the resources and chart their and your progress!

1. Parents Self-Rating Chart

2. Daily Child's Play Progress Record Chart

3. A list of First 100 Words children learn

BONUS #2

5 Day Training Course

1. Does your toddler understand basic instructions?

2. Are they able to let you know what they want and need?

3. Do you know how to help your toddler understand your simple instructions?

If you answered 'no' to any or all of the above questions, then you need this **FREE 5-day video training course**.

Simply click the link below – sign up with your email and start receiving one link a day over 5 days.

Follow the strategies and see the progress – let me know how it goes😊

BONUS #3

Potty Training Tips

As we all know, children with delayed speech and language development learn better with visual aids. I have created a step-by-step potty-training strip with words and pictures, which you can stick on the bathroom wall or your living room or both!

The steps include:

- Pulling down each item of clothing
- Sitting on the potty
- Pulling all clothes up
- Emptying the potty into the toilet
- Washing hands

These step-by-step instructions will make it easier and fun to explain/show to your child.

To access this FREE resource, pleas click on the link below:

https://kidssltessentials.com/coping-skills-for-kids/

INTRODUCTION

Emotions are a tricky business and adults naturally assume that because of our age, we completely have the skill of emotional regulation under control. But do we really? Think about the last time something emotional happened to you. It could be good or bad but you were desperate to express them but instead, you had to keep them bottled up.

I will share my example with you. Overall, I think I am quite a calm person but what may seem trivial to others drives me crazy— manners! A few weeks back, the first job of the day was to queue at the post office. Knowing how busy it would be, I left as early as possible, sacrificing my first cup of tea of the day. Minding my own business, a sweet old lady queue-jumped but looked at me with an innocent smile and as she turned away, a smirk developed.

I was furious as I believe in respecting elders but she played me like a fiddle! And of course, I couldn't say anything. My blood boiled for the drive home and the first thing I did when one of my daughters asked me a question, I snapped. Through no fault of hers, my bottled-up emotions slipped out.

Does this sound familiar? Now go back to the last ten times you had a strong emotion you wanted to share. Would you say that half the time, you kept it all inside, or is it more like 80 to 90 percent of the time?

Now, look at your little one. Bearing in mind they don't have the same 20+plus years of experience we do, it's understandable how they have the same emotional problems we do. These tiny human beings don't have the ability to identify their emotions and they certainly aren't capable of expressing them appropriately.

What we as adults seem to forget is that just as we don't enjoy our emotional outbursts, neither do children. Furthermore, if we react negatively to their outbursts, we are only fighting fire with fire, making them feel worse!

At such a young age, toddlers and young children are only beginning to learn how to express themselves verbally. They don't have the vocabulary or the language skills to accurately express a feeling that they can't quite pinpoint.

This leads to frustration and lashing out. You may notice toddlers having temper tantrums as well as other bad behaviour that causes you to panic. We aren't unrealistic and we know that our children aren't perfect and as parents, there is an awful lot to learn. But this doesn't stop us from feeling terrible every time our children get themselves worked up into an emotional state.

Considering how important the early years are, it's no wonder that your concerns aren't just about now, but also about their future.

"The reality is that most of us communicate the same way we grew up. That communication style becomes our normal way of dealing with issues, our blueprint for communication. It's what we know and pass on to our own children. We either become our childhood or we make a conscious choice to change it."

— KRISTEN CROCKETT

As children, we look to role models for emotional awareness. It's not a case of blaming our parents for our emotional issues. As children, we learn from all of our care providers including extended family, teachers, and friends. This emotional baggage is a motivation for making sure your children don't grow up the same way our generation generally has— suppressing our feelings and forcing positivity.

How much simpler would your life be if you could effectively communicate your emotions, whether that's with your children, your partner, and your co-workers? Isn't this one of the best life skills you could teach your child?

In this book, we are going to dive into the science of emotional intelligence for children, recognise different emotions, and learn how to manage them in a healthy way. We will learn how to listen to our children even when their verbal communication isn't fully developed, and how to better understand children through their body language.

Though my other books have touched on how to handle big emotions, this book will take understanding to a new level with mindfulness strategies, games, and play therapy. While the goal is to help your little one with emotional regulation, your learning will help you to develop your own skills so that your parent-child relationship is stronger and healthier.

What is special about this book is that the activities aren't only going to benefit your child. The first 90 activities are aimed at children while the final chapter is dedicated to helping you and your journey towards emotional regulation.

Aside from my own three children, I have been working as a speech and language therapist for almost 20 years now. Though my primary objective is to help children with a range of social and learning delays and disorders, it's hard not to connect with parents and support them through their struggles.

I couldn't help but feel that my job limited me to the number of children and parents that I could help, which led me to write various books on topics like autism, speech and language development, and activity books to encourage play. From there, I started our wonderful Facebook community, *Kids' Delayed Speech and Language Support Group*, which now has more than 7,300 members kindly sharing their experiences and offering more advice. And last year, I launched my course for parents, *Toddler Chat*.

Where ever possible, I try to offer as much free help as I can. Don't forget to check out the link at the beginning of the book to get some samples!

All of these adventures haven't just been about sharing my professional and personal experiences. It's been about learning from parents in order to provide the right techniques and strategies to make life easier for families.

So far, it's been a heart-warming pleasure to have met so many people and this is what motivates me to keep reassuring parents that they have all it takes to help their children develop all the skills they need to thrive as they start school, develop friendships, go through secondary education, into their careers and well into adulthood.

Parenting is the most rewarding job in the world, but as I have said many times, it's also the most difficult. You never feel like you are getting it right and when you do make progress, it seems that there is a giant step back. It does mean that with the right guidance, you can start feeling confident about your parenting skills and enjoy this amazing role!

I want to take this opportunity to thank everyone who has left reviews for my previous books as the feedback helps me create content that will benefit the many. It also gives me a chance to hear feedback and make improvements. I am grateful to those who have mentioned the spelling mistakes but as I am based in the UK, I write in British English. American readers, please forgive the Ss and the Us that we use on the other side of the pond.

Before we get started with developing your child's emotional awareness, let's get a better understanding of what exactly emotional intelligence is.

1

EMOTIONAL INTELLIGENCE—WHAT'S THE BIG DEAL?

"Emotional intelligence begins to develop in the earliest years. All the small exchanges children have with their parents, teachers, and with each other carry emotional messages."

— DANIEL GOLEMAN

For many years, the focus was on intelligence quotient or IQ. People became somewhat obsessed with putting a number on their reasoning and problem-solving abilities. IQ scores have been used to measure academic abilities, educational placements, and to spot the "gifted". It has been considered a gauge for job recruiters, even by the police and the military. More recently, we have discovered the problem with focusing on IQ!

WHAT IS EMOTIONAL INTELLIGENCE

Emotional intelligence (EQ and also known as EI) is the same for everyone, regardless of age. It's the ability to recognise, identify, and control emotions in oneself and to accurately identify the emotions of others and respond appropriately. It's true that while the definition is the same for everyone, not everyone has the same levels of skill when it comes to emotional management.

Aside from the labelling and controlling of emotions, EQ deals with the awareness of your own strengths and weaknesses, confidence, the ability to let go of mistakes, and the ability to accept change. More specifically, EQ can be described as having five elements; self-awareness, self-regulation, motivation, empathy, and social skills.

- Self-awareness- this is the part that covers understanding feelings and why you are having them. It's also important to understand the impact your emotions have on others. Self-awareness helps us to make the right decisions based on our intuition.
- Self-regulation- this element helps us to manage those emotions, especially the ones that can lead to

negative consequences. It requires learning calming techniques rather than burying emotions.
- Motivation- motivation helps you to see you are capable of learning new things and bettering yourself. It's about optimising your experiences, seizing opportunities, and becoming more resilient.
- Empathy- here, we don't only consider other people's feelings but we think about how this makes them feel. It's about listening to both the verbal and non-verbal cues people give you and respecting other people's opinions in this very diverse world.
- Social skills- social skills include sharing, cooperation, following instructions, eye contact, showing patience, and respecting others and their boundaries.

As an adult, you might be able to recognise some elements that you have mastered. Going back to my queue-jumping granny, I knew I was angry and I managed to use my best social skills, but I also recognise that my self-regulation could have been better.

It's also possible that you can see some of these skills in your child already. Think about a time that you may have hurt yourself and they came over to give you a kiss. Or the time they shared their bruised and dribbled-on banana with you? It's not perfect, but the foundations are there.

EQ vs IQ

There has been much debate over which is more important, the measure of "brain intelligence" over "heart intelligence". IQ tests have been used to assess someone's ability to use logic to solve problems, plan, understand abstract ideas, and grasp and use language.

The problem is, human intelligence is far more complex than just these two types of intelligence and traditional IQ tests didn't encompass the full range of our intelligence.

For example, it's all very well being able to solve a complex algebra problem, but what good is that if you can't relate to the room you are trying to explain it to? This is why IQ is no longer seen as the main determinant of success.

One of the leaders in emotional intelligence, Daniel Goleman believes that EQ can matter even more than IQ. While IQ might help you get a job, without the elements of emotional intelligence, it's going to be hard to keep that job! This is because EQ has a huge impact on our relationships.

What's more, a higher EQ can be better for your health. This is because managing emotions help to reduce stress and stress can lead to a number of mental and physical problems.

It's not to say that intelligence and book smarts aren't important, but the benefits of emotional intelligence can have a greater effect on different areas of life. And this isn't just for adults.

THE BENEFITS OF EQ FOR CHILDREN

Let's begin on a social level. Social skills for young children are crucial because this is what is laying the way for their friendships at preschool and then school. If we look at sharing as one example, children who learn how to share early on will have fewer problems sharing toys, taking turns in games, and interrupting others when speaking.

A child who can't share is going to have difficulties playing with others, not just with friends but also with other children in the family. They are more likely to have behavioural outbursts. Essentially, they aren't going to be very happy. The risk of them becoming the bully or being bullied increases.

To succeed in school, children need emotional intelligence. Carolyn MacCann, Ph.D. and her colleagues compared data from over 160 studies involving 27 countries and 42,000 students. The results should that students with higher emotional intelligence tended to get higher grades, and this was across all age groups (Science Daily, 2019). Children are also more likely to stay in school rather than get left behind and drop out.

When this starts to happen, things can spiral out of control rather quickly. It's normal for children to pair together with those who are in a similar situation. Before long, children, and more so teens, can find themselves making the wrong decisions and ending up with unethical behaviours, even criminal activities.

In summary, children with higher EQ are better at paying attention, they are more engaged at school because of their positive relationships with friends and teachers, and they are more empathetic, making life at home smoother. Children who have higher EQ grow up to be adults with higher EQ and can enjoy more fulfilling relationships, experience less stress in their careers, and achieve more success.

EMOTIONAL INTELLIGENCE CAN BE LEARNT

You may look at your little one and think they are too young to learn how to regulate their emotions. From the moment they were born, they began looking at your facial expressions and listening to your tone of voice to detect emotions. Just because they can't explain what anger feels like or what caused them to get angry, it doesn't mean they aren't able to start learning.

You may also feel that you aren't capable of changing old habits. Thanks to the latest research in neuroplasticity, we now know that the brain is able to learn new things well into adulthood with enough practice.

You want to begin by looking at your own parenting style. There are four parenting styles that impact emotional intelligence. A disapproving style is when a parent punishes what we see as negative emotions. This means that when a child is angry, they might get a time-out or have a toy taken away from them. Anger isn't a negative emotion, there are no negative emotions because they are all there for a reason. Their reaction to anger might not have been ideal, but they won't distinguish the difference between the emotion and reaction and your punishment, meaning they will assume the punishment is because they were angry.

On the other hand, some parents have a dismissive style, where they don't validate their child's feelings. I'm sure I'm not the only one to confess to this but if a child is crying, a dismissive parent will tell them there is no need to cry, in the hope that they stop. For an adult, it might not be a reason to cry, but for them, there is normally a genuine reason for their tears.

A step up from this is the Laisssez-faire style, a parent who accepts the entire spectrum of emotions but won't step in to help resolve a problem. The ultimate parenting style is emotion coaching. Parents are patient when children try to express how they feel and see these moments as a chance to get closer, even a chance to learn together.

The entire book is dedicated to strategies that will help children develop their emotional awareness but it's important to know that you don't need any special qualifications or training. Even starting now, you can find dozens of everyday moments to start introducing emotions to children.

When you are reading books, watching cartoons, or playing in the park, start observing more with your little one. Label what you see with sentences like "The dog looks happy." and "I think the man looks sad.".

Don't be afraid to talk about your emotions and the emotions of others in the home. It's ok to say that you are a little bit grumpy because you are tired. Remember, the emotion grumpy isn't bad as long as you aren't taking it out on others. Or celebrate that you are really excited because you have special plans at the weekend.

There are two acronyms that can help you to remember more about emotional intelligence. The first comes from Dr. Marc Brackett, the Director of the Yale Center for Emotional Intelligence, and is RULER:

- R- Recognising emotions in self and others
- U- Understanding the causes and consequences of emotions
- L- labelling emotions accurately
- E- Expressing emotions appropriately
- R- Regulating emotions effectively

(Firestone, 2016)

The second is the CARS technique but rather than helping you to remember the elements of emotional intelligence, it guides you on what to do when children have extremely intense emotional reactions.

- C- Connect: listen, understand, and empathize
- A- Alternative solutions: walk children through the problem-solving process
- R- Respond: respond in a BIFF manner (Brief, Informative, Friendly, Firm)
- S- Set limits: limits instill boundaries so they know their reactions aren't appropriate

(My Mood, My Choices, 2019)

Whether you are trying to regulate your own emotions or better understand your child's, it's helpful to remember that each emotion has a unique purpose. Joy gives us a sense of purpose and improves our well-being whereas sadness slows us down so we can concentrate on the matter at hand. Anger means someone has done wrong to us and kicks us into action. Fear and disgust keep us from danger, harm, and things that are unhealthy.

YOUR CHILD IS A SPONGE

This is the perfect opportunity to think about how much children are constantly observing others, and more specifically, the most important people in their world—you! We tend to worry that our children don't listen to us. There are obviously cases when they really aren't listening but for the most, they are taking in every word you say and how you say it.

Aside from listening to us, children are the kings and queens of observation, soaking in all they see like a sponge. In 1961, the Bobo Doll experiment was carried out on boys and girls from the Stanford University Nursery School involving 72 children aged 3 to 6. The children were rated on their levels of aggression.

Some children were exposed to aggressive toys, others to non-aggressive toys, and then there was a control group. In some cases, the adult used a hammer and others threw the doll in the air and shouted aggressive words. They were exposed to aggressive and non-aggressive behaviour from both male and female adults. Those children who observed the aggressive behaviour from adults were more aggressive than the other groups when testing their levels after observations (McLeod, 2014).

It's not only aggressive behaviour that children will copy. Even as babies, they copy our sounds with their babbling. They watch how we tap away on our phones and tablets. It's frustrating when your toddler responds to everything with a "No", but where do you think they got that from?

At the same time, they are able to copy all of our good emotional and social examples. Letting them see you calm down when you are frustrated is a valuable learning opportunity. Saying please and thank you, and sharing are things that children may feel are things they have to do. So to see an adult doing the same is a fine example!

CHILDREN WHO MAY HAVE EXTRA DIFFICULTIES WITH EMOTIONAL INTELLIGENCE

A child's environment is going to impact their emotional intelligence and social skills and not only because of the example you set as a parent. Childhood trauma can have an effect on a child's emotional development and we shouldn't assume that this is limited to physical violence. There is violence in schools, communities, and wars. There are more natural disasters too. The pandemic had a negative impact on EQ, intrapersonal, interpersonal, and adaptability scales (Martín-Requejo & Santiago-Ramajo, 2021).

Those on the autism spectrum can show excellent intelligence when it comes to problem-solving and logic but many will also have difficulties with social interactions and emotional regulation. Children with ADHD might not be paying enough attention to social cues to pick up on them. Others that have auditory processing disorders, verbal, and non-verbal learning disabilities may also struggle to pick up on social cues, so they don't get the same exposure to examples.

The first thing to remember before helping your child manage their emotions is that every child's brain is different and that means they think and learn in unique ways. They can all get better at the five elements of emotional intelligence (self-awareness, self-regulation, motivation, empathy, and social skills) but they might do so at a different pace than other children. Others may need more help and a wider range of strategies and there will be some that need a little extra patience. But it will always be worth it in the end.

The next question that will probably spring to mind is how do you know if your child's emotional development is normal? First, there is no such thing as "normal" when it comes to child development. Nevertheless, it is useful to know what is typical and atypical in child development. Typical development refers to the progress of a child with respect to the progress of children in the same age group. Atypical refers to those children who either lag behind but may also jump ahead in some areas.

This is where the mum in me kicks in! Even though my children are pretty much all grown up now, I can still remember those younger years and worrying that they were falling behind on every milestone! In the next chapter, we are going to cover the typical milestones in relation to emotional development. This isn't to cause you any panic and if your child doesn't reach a milestone by an exact age, it doesn't mean they won't. However, as early intervention is crucial for children, it's sensible to bring up any concerns you may have with your child's doctor.

Let's take a look at these milestones and what can be done at each stage so that you have a better understanding.

2

EMOTIONAL DEVELOPMENT MILESTONES

At first, the thought of helping your child with their emotional development is a daunting one but when you discover that the majority of it is through play and games, it becomes quite exciting. Nevertheless, before the excitement carries you away, it's essential to know their limitations. Just as a child can't run before they can walk, or write their name before they can hold a pencil, you can't expect them to empathise with your emotions if they aren't at the stage where they can differentiate between their own feelings.

DEFINING SOCIAL AND EMOTIONAL DEVELOPMENT

In the previous chapter, we defined emotional intelligence but there is a massive leap from the child who won't stop screaming because peas are green and not blue to a child who can use techniques to calm themselves down. This process is known as emotional development.

This is a gradual process that starts with recognising emotions in others before labelling simple emotions such as happy, sad, and angry. As they get a little older, they grasp the more complex emotions for their stage of development, such as fear and jealousy. While the greatest challenge is often to control their temper, children also need to develop their control over emotions such as happiness, excitement, and love.

Based on this definition of emotional growth, the link between emotional development and social development is clear to see. The more social experiences a child has in their younger years, the more emotional interactions they will have.

The connection is so important that it is often referred to as social-emotional development. When children have opportunities to develop their social-emotional skills, they begin to understand who they are, how to feel about others and act towards them, and how to create positive relationships and maintain them. All of this is helped by the ability to recognise and manage their emotions.

Overall, social-emotional development allows children to develop speech and language skills and with these skills, they have the tools to practice conflict resolution. Children who have stronger relationships at school with friends and teachers are less likely to struggle academically, even at a young age. Together, all of these skills encourage confidence and self-esteem.

THE 3 MAJOR EMOTIONAL STAGES IN CHILDHOOD DEVELOPMENT

I find it always helps to understand how children develop all of their skills by starting with a little knowledge of how the brain works. In the first five years of a child's life, the brain develops more than at any other time. When a baby is born, the brain is around a quarter of the size of an adult's brain, doubling in the first year of their life. By 5 years old, the brain is at 90 percent of its full size.

We are born with all the brain cells, or neurons, we will have for our entire life. This information leads us to assume that we can't increase the number of brain cells and therefore, we can't "get smarter". What leads to new learning is the connections that are made between the neurons. These connections are called synapses.

Children take in their interactions through their senses and these interactions cause brain cells to fire together to create a connection. The more times neurons fire together, the stronger the connection, so much so that the connections can last a lifetime. Let's put this in perspective.

One of the most common childhood experiences that we have is visiting our grandparents' house. It could be the smell of the cooking, a game you used to play, or even their pet. For me, it was the smell of prathas (Indian flatbread with lots of butter and sugar sprinkled on!). If I had only smelt that pratha a handful of times, the neurons wouldn't have created a strong enough connection to burn the memory of that smell into my brain.

All interactions cause new synapses to grow and for other synapses to become stronger. This all sounds very beautiful but there is a downside. For some, it's not the smell of someone's cooking. It's the experience of unkindness, distance, and a lack of love that are sealed in these synapses.

This is why what we do as parents in the very early years is so important for a child's social-emotional development. Positive interactions stay with children, leading to healthier and happier teenage and adult years. Negative interactions, sadly, will have a lasting effect on a child's emotional intelligence.

Erik Erikson, Developmental Psychologist, coined the 8 stages of psychosocial development. These stages include:

1. Trust vs. mistrust
2. Autonomy vs. shame and doubt
3. Initiative vs. guilt
4. Industry vs. inferiority
5. Identity vs. confusion
6. Intimacy vs. isolation
7. Generativity vs. stagnation
8. Integrity vs. despair

This list is far too extensive for us as stage 1 begins at birth and takes us all the way to retirement age. In fact, the first three stages relate to children up to the age of five. But it is interesting to see how professionals recognise that development is a lifelong experience.

Our focus is on the early years and at this point, I don't want to look at the specific ages. Instead, we will discover the logical order in which emotions develop.

Major Stage 1: Noticing

The first stage of emotional development is noticing all that is going on around them. They are taking in our facial expressions, tone of voice, and attitude to situations. They can pick up on our mood and how we respond to their attempts at getting our attention. Nobody is really sure how many emotions babies are born with. Some believe it's only three: happiness, anger, and fear. As there is only cooing and crying, we don't know the extent of the emotional range.

Major Stage 2: Expressing

Emotions can also be expressed with facial expressions and body language, again, mainly from what they have observed from others. You may also notice things like clapping or throwing things before they start to use vocabulary to express simple emotions. The expressing stage can be challenging because the child's range of emotions grows faster than their ability to express them. This is what happens when children get frustrated and collapse into a tantrum. They have the feeling but not the ability to express it.

Major Stage 3: Managing

This is normally a time when children are finding a little bit of independence and discovering that parents aren't always going to be there to solve problems. There could be new social environments where they have to listen, take turns, share, and use their own words to resolve problems. They need to develop new coping skills and a lot of this comes from managing their emotions.

For children to work through the stages with as much ease as possible, they need to know they are in a safe environment. Think about what it's like when you tell another adult that you feel upset when they treat you in a certain way and they tell you that you are being dramatic, exaggerating, or imagining it. When we tell another adult that they are imagining their feelings, it's called gaslighting. But for some reason, it's normal to do this with children.

Instead of telling them there is no need to cry or that getting angry won't solve anything, show that you understand. Use sentences like "That must have been upsetting. I would have been upset too" so that they know it's okay to have these big emotions.

In the next section, we will begin to look at emotional milestones for different ages but once again, don't panic if it takes your little one 13 months to reach a 12-month milestone. And be humble if your child reaches a milestone earlier. As much as we want to talk about how amazing our children are, remember there will be some parents who are genuinely worried about their child's progress and a little bit of empathy will go a long way.

EMOTIONAL MILESTONES FOR BABIES

The first three months of a baby's life must be crazy! They have gone from this warm, dark place with the sound of their mum's heartbeat to comfort them to a bright world with new sights and sounds on a daily basis. This is very much a noticing stage as their eyesight starts to get clearer. At this age, they will start to understand how humans provide comfort and security. Being picked up or just being around familiar people can reassure them and calm them down. There might be signs of a smile or face pulling when talking to them.

Between 3 and 6 months babies discover their hands and are able to explore things with them. You might see signs of excitement as they wave their arms around in little outbursts. These movements are attempts to communicate with you. Their smile will be obvious and they will begin to laugh too. At the same time, they will learn that crying or fussing is their way to communicate discomfort.

From 6 to 9 months, babies are getting better at expressing more emotions but this is also a crucial stage for observation as they learn from you. They will understand what an angry face means or a louder voice is and may respond to this. Games like peek-a-boo are a great source of entertainment and they might also start to understand the concept of possession, crying when toys are taken away. This is the stage where babies might begin to self-soothe by sucking on thumbs, fingers, or fists.

Just before their first birthday, babies will start to favour different games, toys, and activities. And while they are good at expressing happiness and excitement with these activities, they also have no problems expressing frustration and anger when things don't go their way. It's normal to feel some cooperation from your little one and other moments where there is a complete lack of cooperation. At this age, they may also start looking for your validation and this is essential for healthy self-esteem.

The first year is often the most challenging for parents in terms of emotional development. Between the tantrums and going quiet, retreating inwards, and so much learning, it's hard to see if this is just typical development or if there's a problem. There are some signs of concern though.

If you introduce your baby to a new person, it's natural that they will show signs of discomfort, maybe even fear but this should fade away once back in the comfort of your arms. If they continue to show signs of discomfort, difficulty sleeping, or not wanting to eat, just make note of this in case it happens again. You might notice the same reaction when taking your baby to a new environment.

In some cases, babies' emotions can be so much for them and this can lead to stress. This seems hard to believe that babies can be that stressed but this can manifest in physical symptoms. If you notice your baby is particularly lethargic, especially when you introduce a new toy or game and there is little to no interest, this is another thing to make a note of.

In all cases, all of this might be perfectly normal and there is no need to rush to the doctor. But if you have concerns, you can bring them up at the next medical review.

EMOTIONAL MILESTONES FOR TODDLERHOOD

Starting with older babies, at this stage they will start to make connections between someone's facial expressions and tone of voice. The relationship with their primary caregivers strengthens but they also recognise that they are separate from them and this encourages them to explore more of the world around them.

When upset, older babies will still self-soothe but you might find them distracting themselves through play. This is when little ones learn that their main caregiver can't always be there for them. Nevertheless, by responding to your little one as quickly as possible, the better they become at understanding and managing their feelings.

The toddler stage is when children can start naming some of their basic emotions and they will continue to learn more about emotions through play. As well as their play becoming more independent, there will be other signs of independence that might come as a shock to you.

Toddlers often only see things from their point of view. If you add this to the limited ability to express their feelings accurately, extreme behaviour changes can be sudden. A temper tantrum can return to perfect calm before you have even had time to work out what the issue is.

It takes a lot of effort from adults not to respond to anger and frustration with the same emotions. If you need to take a moment to get your emotions in check do so because this is the best example you can set.

Toddlers appreciate cuddles, stroking, patting, and other actions that have a soothing, calming effect on them. With our busy lives, sometimes they just need a quiet comfortable place to give their senses a rest.

They will enjoy opportunities to play with you and talk to you about their play. These moments are invaluable because they offer you the chance to see things from their perspective.

If your child is showing no signs of emotional awareness, for example, they don't react when you are upset or they don't clap their hands or smile when they are happy, make a note to talk to your doctor. Also, although toddlers have mood swings, they shouldn't occur with such a frequency that you find yourself struggling to cope. Keep an eye out for sleep disturbances or difficulty concentrating too.

EMOTIONAL MILESTONES FOR PRE-SCHOOLERS

These are exciting times in terms of emotional development. It's normally the age when most children start some form of preschool or nursery. This means that on the one hand, they have to learn about separation from their main caregivers and this can cause a lot of anxiety for some children.

On the other hand, this is also the time when they start to play with other children and for some, this could be the first time they have actually spent a significant amount of time with other people their age. In these moments, children get to see how other children express their emotions and they start to use more words when talking about their own.

You will notice that their range of emotions increases, in particular, they will start to develop empathy. It's possible that they will tell you about a friend who was crying or upset in preschool. You may also see empathy in their play. They might be more interested in taking care of dolls or characters that are in need.

With regards to expressing their emotions, there will also be advancements, especially with the right role models. Instead of getting upset and grumpy when they are tired, they will be able to tell you. There will still be moments of frustration and anger but rather than the toddler tantrums that appeared more aggressive, like throwing things, you will be able to see the changes in mood by their facial expressions or actions like stomping the ground.

This is also the age when children start to develop fears. These fears could be very real, dogs, thunderstorms, etc., or they could be related to the world of their imagination, such as ghosts and monsters under the bed. It's important to validate their feelings. Even though the monster isn't real, their emotions are.

In terms of 'new' emotions, pride and shame are two that will start to appear. Children around this age will look for signs of appraisal from parents when they complete certain tasks and will take pride in their achievements. It's essential that you foster this so that their confidence can continue to grow. If they can't complete their intended activity, they might express their disappointment and shame through sadness, possibly even anger.

Changes in routine can be a shock at this age, especially for those who haven't attended any form of early education. This can add to the difficulties they already face with separation anxiety. On the other hand, you might notice children pushing you away. This might seem like a heavy stab in the back but it's actually a good sign. They are trying to express their independence.

As time goes on and they settle into the new preschool routine, emotions will start to settle down again. You may notice that there is less focus on rules because they are learning their limits. They will begin to understand concepts like "mine", "yours" and "theirs" which makes turn-taking and sharing a lot easier. They will become more used to being apart from you and start to seek out other children to play with. Nevertheless, changes in the routine can upset them.

EMOTIONAL MILESTONES FOR 5 TO 6-YEAR-OLDS

As you might imagine, emotions at this age may well depend on whether or not they have attended preschool. The transition from preschool to primary school is easier on a child's emotions because they have an understanding of what to expect. If they haven't been to preschool, you may notice signs of separation anxiety and they might process this more internally, becoming quiet, almost shy.

The new school routine could lead to added tiredness, depending on the hours they were at preschool for. Even as adults, we know that managing emotions is harder when exhausted, so don't be surprised if there seems to be a little regression in how they handle their emotions while they are adapting to the longer days.

Children at this age are often learning 5 to 10 new words each day. If you have ever tried to learn a new language, you can understand how impressive this is. Because of this, you will be able to hear children using more complex sentences, even sounding like mini-adults.

This immense amount of new vocabulary helps children of this age express their emotions better though they may struggle with expressing emotions like jealousy and differentiating between anger and frustration.

Play and friendship are increasingly important. There is a greater need to be liked by friends and they might try to be more like their friends. They will be more aware of the rules in play however the rules of some games might be a challenge for them. With other children, there will be more cooperation. Children might plan together how to achieve something, like building with bricks.

One thing that many parents find quite pleasing is the ability to show more patience. Children of this age still have needs that have to be met but they are better at waiting for their requirements. As they continue to become more independent, they may try to find solutions to meet their own needs. This may happen before this age depending on family situations like having a younger sibling.

Speaking of independence, this is the age when some children might like to make some of their own decisions. They may enjoy picking out their own clothes or making a choice about meals. Allowing them to do so will help them with problem-solving skills later on in life.

Despite this independence and the fun they have playing with friends, children at this age still need their parents for love, support, and quality time together. This is the time when children get to talk to you about their feelings, fears, and needs, It's also a chance for you to show your approval and praise achievements, which is still like gold dust for them.

HOW TO FOSTER EMOTIONAL DEVELOPMENT THROUGHOUT THE EARLY YEARS

In the final section of this chapter, we will look at different ways to help children with their emotional development. Don't forget that taking time, even if it's just 5 minutes a day as I always say, to help with emotional development, you will also help in other areas of development. The time you spend with your little one helps with vocabulary and language development, social skills, and increasing confidence. Let's look back at the different ages, starting with babies.

Enjoying time with your baby

Begin by making sure your baby is in a safe and secure environment, one that is consistent and allows them to feel confident. This is the best age to lay the foundations of their emotional development. This can be helped with routine!

Give your baby plenty of physical contact. Don't fall victim to the old-school theory of spoiling your baby with love. A study has shown that extra carrying of babies reduces crying and fuss by 43 percent. Furthermore, babies were less fussy during the evening by 51 percent (Hunziker & Barr, 1986). This could be why babies in western cultures are more likely to suffer from colic compared with other cultures. For example, in Bali, babies are constantly held for the first three months of their lives until the ceremony of the "three moons" or Tiga Bulan. Feet don't touch the earth because, in these first months, babies are considered to be of the heavens.

Being a baby doesn't mean you have to talk to them in "coochee cooes" and other nonsensical words and sounds. You can talk to your baby, sing to them, and read them stories in a positive tone. Respond to their babbling, taking turns at this early stage is the beginning of taking turns in conversations later on in life.

Even at this young age, you can start to name their feelings and acknowledge their different emotions. You can do this during your daily activities but also through play, matching each other's facial expressions and mimicking their tones.

Keeping calm when toddlers can't

Continue to talk about feelings, labelling and validating all of their emotions. This is going to be hard when dealing with anger and tantrums. No matter what, you have to stay calm and this won't be the last time you hear this from me. Always have in mind that they don't have the ability to express how they are feeling and retaliating with your own anger is teaching them that outbursts are acceptable. There are a good number of books and stories that can help you deal with anger and outbursts.

This is an important time to start showing empathy toward your little one and towards others. During those difficult, angry moments, this is the time that you really need to show your understanding. Be there for them whether that's giving them extra hugs and kisses or sitting next to them until they calm down…and they will calm down! The patience you have now will make life easier in the long run.

This is also an amazing time to really engage your children in play in order to help their emotions progress. Puppets, dressing up, and pretend play allow you both to explore your feelings and expand their vocabulary. There are endless games with pretend play and you both get the chance to be creative and imaginative.

Both messy play and outdoor play are good ways to let young children express their feelings and let out emotions that have been building up. Colouring, painting, and drawing are all ways that children can show how they are feeling. When you can see little ones getting upset or frustrated, offering them some colours and a piece of paper can help calm them down.

Try to start using more positive reinforcement than words like "No" and "Don't". Obviously, there is a time and a place for these words but overusing them reduces the impact. Praising the positive encourages more positive behaviour and also gives them opportunities to make you proud!

Don't be afraid to talk about your emotions and take this one step further by explaining why you feel a particular way. It's okay to let children know that you are tired because you have had a long day or that you are upset because someone wasn't nice to you at work.

Supporting pre-schoolers and their big emotions

In the first place, you can continue all that you were doing in the toddler stage for this age too. Children still need opportunities to play and express their feelings, even if they are going to preschool. You can take advantage of things that happen at preschool by asking questions. For example, if your child tells you someone was angry, you can ask why they think they were angry, what had happened to make them angry and then talk about ways they could help their friend.

Start to give your little one opportunities to cope with their big feelings. You can show them how you take deep breaths when you are feeling overwhelmed. You can also encourage them to go to a quiet place if they want to. There is a difference between sending someone for a time-out where they feel punished and suggesting they take a moment of calm.

Providing children with lots of different ways to handle their emotions enables children to take initiative and decide what is right for them. Eventually, children will learn to go to their coping strategy before their big emotions take over.

Games can reinforce skills they need at preschool. There are lots of household chores that can be turned into games for this. You can take turns folding laundry or laying things on the table. Let children help you with the cooking so that they get better at listening to and following instructions.

Make sure you have realistic expectations for children at this age. There might be setbacks and they may even still have temper tantrums. If you expect too much, they might pick up on your disappointment. You still want to have that environment that is safe, secure, and where they have opportunities to try new things, appreciate their capabilities, and build their confidence.

What 5 to 6-year-olds need from you

From here on, it's about maintaining the development you have been working on in the early years. The difference is, you can adapt these skills and make them age appropriate. At this age, they will know the difference between balls to play with and a stress ball you give them as a coping method.

As they start to read, you can choose books with sight words (keywords that frequently appear) especially related to emotions. You can even encourage them to make up their own stories about characters in different situations and the feelings that may arise.

Tasks may become more complex, so teach them how to break things down into smaller, more manageable steps. This will make new challenges easier to achieve so they are still building their confidence and prevent frustration. At the same time, don't make everything too easy. They won't gain a sense of satisfaction from this and they might start to assume you will always be there to solve problems for them.

If there had to be one key takeaway from this chapter, it would be to validate all feelings your child has. I know you are busy and the fact that your child hits the roof because you can't find their Paw Patrol socks is really not a big issue for you, but for them, it's a disaster. Don't let your child grow up as many of us had to only being allowed to show certain feelings. Women have the right to be angry as much as men have the right to cry. Validating emotions in little people will encourage them to grow up with greater emotional intelligence!

If there is one quick way to undo the effort you put into your child's emotional development it's to not listen to them. Imagine they are telling you a story about how a friend hurt them in the playground and you reply with "That's nice darling", they are soon going to learn that there is little point in telling you their important stories.

In the next chapter, we will learn why and how to listen to children before looking at things that may trigger specific moods.

3

LISTENING TO YOUR CHILD

"Listen to your child enough and you will come to realize that he or she is quite an extraordinary individual. And the more extraordinary you realize your child to be the more you will be willing to listen. And the more you will learn."

— M. SCOTT PECK

As parents, one of our main challenges is getting our children to listen to us. I'm not sure how many times I used to say, "Are you listening?" and even though they are teenagers, I still regularly find myself repeating the mantra. The level of attention a child pays to you is almost a sign of your effective parenting. How proud are you when you say something once and your child responds?

Be sure to give yourself a pat on the back because it is amazing when little people with all that is going on around them actually listen. In terms of safety, it is crucial, that children listen. But you are about to discover in this chapter that in terms of emotional development, it's actually your ability to listen to them that can make all the difference.

WHAT IS ACTIVE LISTENING

If we are honest with ourselves, a lot of the time we are passive listeners. Our children talk to us and at the same time we are cooking, responding to an email, or our brains are working through the never-ending to-do list. We might take in their words but the skill stops there.

Active listening is when we listen with all our attention not just to the verbal cues but also to the non-verbal messages children are giving us. Once we have taken in the complete message, without interrupting or giving our opinion mid-story, we are able to respond appropriately. Active listening also involves us showing signs to our children that we are listening with all of our attention.

There are a number of reasons why active listening is beneficial and not just with children. In order to have a meaningful conversation, you need to be able to listen to what the other person is saying before you talk. The moments when you listen are critical is you want to gather as much information as you can about your child and what's happening in their world. Here are some more reasons to work on active listening:

- It builds stronger relationships between you and your little one.
- You are setting a positive, respectful example.
- Active listening is essential for problem-solving.
- Your children often have the answer to their problems or needs if you are able to listen.
- You can't expect your child to listen to you if you aren't listening to them.

The problem most parents will have is a lack of time combined with children's inability to recognise when you are free to listen to them. Even though it might not be the best time for you, ultimately, you will save time if you can stop what you are doing and listen to your child. Not listening can lead to emotional distress later on and this will often take longer to resolve than the few minutes they require at that particular moment.

HOW TO PRACTICE ACTIVE LISTENING WITH YOUR CHILD

As soon as your child shows signs that they want to talk to you, stop what you are doing. These could be verbal signs like calling your name or non-verbal ones such as getting irritated or becoming restless while playing. If they happen to call for you and it's impossible for you to stop what you are doing, let them know that you will finish what you are doing and that you will be right there…and keep your promise!

It really helps to get down to a child's level as this will be easier to make eye contact. You might want to sit on the floor with them or sit on the sofa together. Sitting down makes you appear smaller and less intimidating. This might sound ridiculous, after all, how can a kind and loving parent seem intimidating but if they are nervous about what they want to say, it will help not to stand over them.

One of the hardest parts of active listening is to quiet your mind. Again, we love our children to bits but we also know that some of their stories can go on for a while! During that time, the challenge is to keep your mind focused and not wander off to decide what to have for dinner. Pull your focus back by not only listening to their words but also looking at their facial expressions and gestures as this will tell you a lot as well. Body language is a detailed topic, so we will cover this in a separate chapter.

If you do notice your mind drifting and you miss what they have said, it's okay to be honest. Apologise and admit that you were distracted. In fact, this is far better than bluffing your way out of not paying attention because you are teaching them positive examples.

Aside from active listening, we have a wonderful tool called reflective listening. Reflective listening can come in two forms. First, there are fillers. These are words or sounds that we use at appropriate times during a conversation to show that we are listening. Sometimes, they can be sounds like "Ohhh!" and "Umm!". Others will be words or expressions such as "No way!" or "Really!".

Second, reflective listening can be repeating what they say in order to show you are listening. Imagine your child says "I finded the ball". In return, you would say "You found the ball." Not only have you shown you were listening but you have also had a chance to correct their grammatical mistakes. To take your reflective listening a step further, you can add an adjective before the word ball to expand their vocabulary.

Reflective listening also gives you the chance to talk about emotions. When your child is telling you something or showing signs of emotions, you can reflect on this. You might say something like "It seems you are angry about something." and even if they aren't sure if they are angry, they may decide that they want to talk more about it.

Children aren't afraid to tell their parents when they are wrong and this works to our advantage. Even if you try to guess how they are feeling and make a mistake, they will often correct you. I remember when one of mine was around three and I mentioned that she looked tired. She put me right in my place and told me she wasn't tired, she was angry!

This leads me nicely to children and their moods. It's not always the case that their words tell us everything that is going on. Understanding what triggers a child's mood can help prevent extreme ups and downs.

CHILDREN'S MOODS AND THEIR TRIGGERS

Going back to the dear old lady who jumped the queue in front of me, there is one thing we need to think about before discussing triggers. The question I had to ask myself was "Am I angry because she pushed in front of me or am I angrier at myself?". You may wonder why I would be angry at myself when I didn't break the social rule but on a deeper level, I was angry at myself for not having the tools and the confidence to assertively highlight the lady's wrongdoing.

The same thing happens with children. There is a situation or a feeling that has caused a problem, but it is rarely the problem that causes an emotion. It's their internal dialogues and the thoughts that they have about a problem that cause the emotion. Imagine a child has sat and eaten all of their dinner except their last piece of chicken. They begrudgingly ate their vegetables knowing that they had saved the prize til last. Then along comes their older sibling and eats that last piece of chicken.

The problem isn't necessarily that they are hungry and need that piece of chicken. The problem is that they were proud of themselves for their achievement and their reward has been stolen from them. For this reason, there is a reaction. Triggers are things that cause these reactions.

Triggers can often lead to emotional attacks. In the case of the thieving sibling, a child might burst out with "You are stupid" or "I hate you". These words are often not true but are used because they don't have the tools to handle their feelings.

Don't forget that not all triggers are bad. Feelings of warmth, happiness, and love are triggered by a hug. Tickles trigger laughter. But naturally, it's the triggers that lead to difficult emotional outbursts that we will focus on.

IDENTIFYING YOUR CHILD'S TRIGGERS

Let's take a look at some of the most common triggers we see in our little ones. The first are the triggers that are caused by aversive situations, those that they really dislike. Hunger is a massive trigger. We see this from the moment babies are born. They are hungry, they cry. As babies get older, their tears might be exchanged for moments of grumpiness, anger, or sudden drops in energy. The same can be said for when they are tired and even when they are feeling hot or cold. Don't forget that even thirst can be a trigger!

Anxiety, fear, and pain are three common triggers in little people though their reactions may differ. Someone who is startled by a loud noise may shout or scream. Anxiety or fear brought about by something that isn't sudden (more like a thought or a dream) can make children sad, they may cry, whereas others may withdraw.

These triggers and reactions are perfectly understandable. It's the body's way of expressing needs or protecting itself. At other times, it's not a need but rather things aren't going their way.

Triggers can include certain activities coming to an end when they aren't ready, for example, having to stop playing or the end of screen time. They want to go swimming but you have to go shopping, which triggers annoyance. In some cases, the trigger will be an activity they have to do but don't want to do such as going to bed or going to school, tidying up or any other activity that isn't as fun as what they are doing at the time.

Most of us have probably witnessed what happens when a child loses a game, makes a mistake, or doesn't do as well at something as they had hoped. Frustration triggers an outburst. They might also get frustrated when they have to do something they don't want to, like waiting. And prepare yourself for the potential outburst at the word "No"!

As their relationships develop, whether that's with other adults or friends, a child's sense of injustice also starts to grow. If another person does something wrong, especially if it impacts them, they might get triggered. There would be a huge sense of injustice in the case of the thieving sibling if the child was told off for their outburst while the sibling got away with their behaviour.

You may also see reactions when other children don't share or take turns when someone cheats. Again, there will be different emotional responses but feeling ignored or being left out is a significant injustice too.

In an effort to improve your own emotional intelligence, it's only right that you look at your triggers as well as your child's. Your children, partner, and colleagues can all do things that will trigger you. But bear in mind that we adults tend to have our own pet peeves that can trigger a reaction that others may not deserve.

HOW TO HELP WITH TRIGGER AWARENESS

Much like getting better at managing our own triggers, we first have to know what they are. The first step to helping little people is to identify what is causing their reactions and this requires your power of observation. Watch your child in a number of different situations including play time, time when they are concentrating (homework, puzzles, etc.) and time when they are socializing with friends.

To get a more complete picture, observe them at different times of the day. This is how you will detect aversive triggers like hunger and tiredness. It will be extremely useful if you ask other adults to pay closer attention for a while too, letting you know if they see any patterns. If need be, keep notes of the patterns that you and others notice.

Putting this into context. Imagine we ask a child to do two activities, let's say threading beads onto string and a puzzle. They complete the puzzle with no drama and move on to the threading activity. If they start to get anxious, fidgety, or frustrated, there is a warning sign.

From here, we have options. Because adults don't always see things the same way children do, we can ask questions in order to try and see things from their perspective. Ask them how they were feeling before they started feeling angry. If they are too young to express their emotions, that's okay, we can move on to detective mode number two!

To get a better idea of what the trigger is, we can assume that it was either the activity that they didn't like or it was an aversive trigger, they were starting to feel thirsty and/or needed a break before the next activity, as some examples. The next step would be to change the order of activities, bead threading first, and the puzzle second. If there is no reaction when the activity changes, you know the issue was probably with the activity. This will be an invaluable tool for when your child is older and doing homework. If you notice a change of attitude towards a subject and you have ruled out other triggers, it's a sign that they might be struggling with a particular subject.

If your child is too young to tell you how they are feeling, it will be a process of elimination until you find the trigger. But have faith in your instincts. You probably already know when your little one is getting tired or hungry, you may be able to spot the signs of boredom even before your moments of observation.

Another activity that works well for older children is to have a brainstorming session. Give each person a piece of paper and ask them to write, draw, or just talk about the thing that makes them angry. Make sure you are also talking about your triggers! Once everyone has come up with their ideas, divide the ideas into two lists: situations you can prevent and situations that you can't.

The next step is to talk through some of the triggers so children can see how some situations can be avoided. My favourite is when a toy gets broken or lost and a child gets mad. We can explain that the mad feeling could be prevented if toys get put away properly. In a perfect world, our little ones would never get hurt and while we can do everything in our power to prevent it, sometimes, there will be accidents and it's natural for them to react. In unavoidable situations, you can give them coping strategies, like an emotions wheel to show you how they feel.

It makes sense that the earlier you start talking to children about emotions, the easier for them to talk about how they feel. It doesn't just have to be talking about their emotions, even going for a walk and observing how others might be feeling will encourage children to open up more.

It's not only emotions that you can talk about. Many reactions come with physical symptoms, flushing in the cheeks, they might feel their heart rate and breathing getting faster or tension in the muscles. They may not see a connection between these physical symptoms and their emotional reactions.

Again, it's a process and there will be times when your child may need help connecting the dots. When you see they can't quite work out that A is causing B, use structures like "I see that when _A_ happens, you _B_". When they get better at spotting the connection, they are more prepared for the problem-solving stage and putting their plan into action.

One final behavioural management technique is to teach your child a cue. A cue can be a word, a hand gesture, or another type of sign that they can use when there is a trigger and they can let you know. This works both ways because if you are in a situation and can see a trigger before they do, you can also warn them. Having a little head start can be enough to prepare them. If for some reason, they don't use the cue, or they ignore you when you use it, check-in and find out what happened. Remind them of your plan and what might happen when they don't stick to the plan.

8 KID-POWER EMOTIONAL SAFETY TECHNIQUES FOR ALL AGES

Now that we have identified the triggers, the aim is to reduce or even completely eliminate the emotional outbursts. That's not to say that we should teach children to ignore their feelings. But the following techniques can help to take away the intensity of what they are feeling so that you can talk to each other. These tips aren't age specific and can be adapted so that they are more suitable for your family's needs.

1. Breathing- take some deep breaths and say "I think I need to calm down" so that little ones follow your lead. There will be more on breathing techniques later.
2. Palm pressure- feel more centred by pushing palms together or by placing them on a hard surface like a wall or a table and pushing down.
3. Ditch the painful words- use your arm to make a loop, like the rim of a bin. Teach children how to catch the painful words as they leave their heads and try to get into their hearts where they can stay for longer. Older children can even write the words down, screw up the paper and aim to throw them in the bin.
4. Mighty power- many of their favourite superheroes have specific powers and mottos to go with them. Imagine how Spidey uses his Spidey power and

creates webs. Teach children how to use their special power to create a protective shield around them so that painful words from others can't enter.

5. Reducing the power of words- for every harsh or hateful word that springs to mind, follow it with a positive. Examples might include "Ugly - ice cream", "Stupid - sun", or "fat - toys". It has to be words that make them feel happy in order to reduce the pain of the hurtful words.

6. Waterproofing the skin- like the superpower, children put on a raincoat or a special cream that waterproofs their skin so that hurtful words can't get through.

7. Call out the lie- This works as much for when children say hurtful things to you as when other children insult them. Without any anger or bitterness, simply say "That's not true". Note that it's not the same as saying "That's a lie". The second statement implies the other person is a liar and they might retaliate.

8. Reassure and take a break- This is often more appropriate for older children, teens, and adults, people of an age where they need time to process what has been said and their feelings. Reassure them with "I love you" and follow it up with "but we will talk about this later when we are calmer". Another example would be "You are important to me and I

care about you, but I'm going to walk away for a bit and come back".

Taking away the emotion behind a trigger calms the body and the mind for all involved. This enables people to reassess the situation and the options that are available and in the end, make better decisions.

A final strategy to help children understand anger and other powerful emotions is the use the iceberg tool. We know how the tip of the iceberg is all that we can see. This tip represents our anger. The mass of ice below holds the triggers of the anger.

My ______________ Iceberg

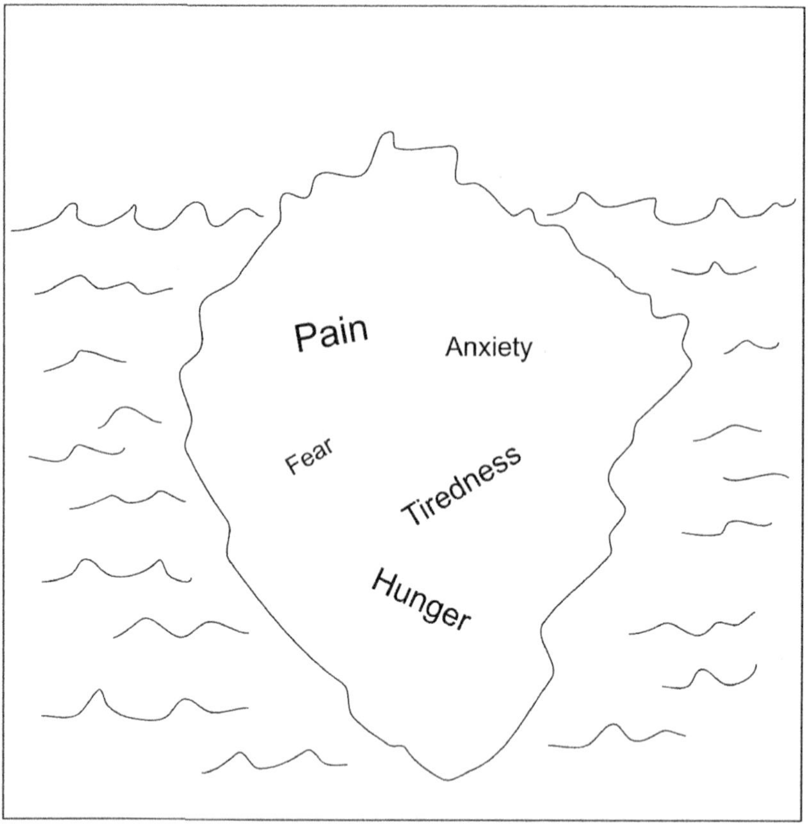
Pain
Anxiety
Fear
Tiredness
Hunger

This won't be the first time that I confess to my terrible drawing skills but you get the idea! Depending on the age of the child, you can write words below the surface of the water, draw pictures, or cut images from magazines. Anything that pops into their mind about the potential triggers of their reaction. Ninety per cent of an iceberg is what can't be seen and only 10 per cent is what is seen. To solve a problem, it's not about the 10 per cent reaction, it's what we can't see!

"Problems cannot be solved with the same mind set that created them."

— ALBERT EINSTEIN

Your child is constantly trying to tell you things but in their own unique way. Sometimes, you can look at them and know straight away what is going on. As emotions start to get more complicated, what they say and how they act won't match or they aren't sure exactly what is going on inside and how to tell you.

In these moments, it will be down to your listening and observing skills that will allow you to begin to decipher what is really going on. Once you have a better idea of what is triggering their emotional outbursts, whether avoidable or not, you can begin to help them connect the dots between the problem, the reaction, and potential solutions.

This poor old lady who jumped the queue deserves a dedication page but she taught me such a valuable lesson about my own emotional management that her behaviour is relevant. As I mentioned, perhaps my anger came from frustration with myself not having the tools to deal with her queue jumping. Another reason for emotional outbursts is that our boundaries have been broken— a very significant trigger for all ages!

4

THE IMPORTANCE OF SETTING HEALTHY BOUNDARIES

"Children raised with good boundaries learn that they are not only responsible for their lives, but also free to live their lives any way they choose, as long as they take responsibility for their choices. For the responsible adult, the sky is the limit."

— HENRY CLOUD

The funny thing about boundaries is that we all know what they are. We know that there is a limit between something we are happy and comfortable with and when someone or something goes too far and you are now uncomfortable. What we aren't always clear about is where that line is. What fewer people are able to do is set their boundaries and how to make sure people respect them. Like so many things in life, the best way to teach children about something is to show them. When children see that you have boundaries and there are consequences for crossing them, they have the role model for their own boundaries—assuming you are getting it right!

WHAT ARE PERSONAL BOUNDARIES

Personal boundaries are the rules that we set within relationships and a guide to how we would like people to treat us. Boundaries are based on our core beliefs, values, and ethics. Boundaries can be related to personal space, your sense of humour, or the amount of pressure and stress you can handle. Your boundaries can change depending on who you are dealing with. If you take personal space as an example, you may be more than comfortable with a hug from your best friend but you aren't the type of person to hug people that you have just met.

Boundaries are essential for relationships and our own mental health but only when they are healthy. Healthy boundaries let us stand up for ourselves with confidence, express our opinions, and recognise our limits in different areas of our lives.

When boundaries become too rigid, people may struggle to develop close relationships because they can't express their thoughts and feelings honestly. They can withdraw and close themselves off from others. On the contrary, porous boundaries allow others to take advantage, some knowingly, others not. People with porous boundaries may struggle to say no, they can take on too many responsibilities, and it often feels like they are carrying the weight of the world on their shoulders.

Aside from the quality of our boundaries, there are also types. Material boundaries deal with our possessions. These can start early on in life with toys, teenage siblings need boundaries when it comes to borrowing each other's things. For adults, it can be anything from lending our car to someone to sharing your Netflix account.

Physical boundaries are necessary for adults and children alike. Some people feel the need for a boundary when it comes to their personal space, others have limits with physical contact. In certain cultures, physical contact is determined by religion or the culture itself. Children need to learn to respect physical boundaries but it's equally important that they learn how to stand up for their own. You would never force yourself to hug and kiss someone you don't want to, regardless of who it is. Children shouldn't be forced to hug or kiss anyone either, even if it is dear Aunt Bessy who is dangling a chocolate bar in the hope of affection.

The third type of boundary is mental boundaries or intellectual boundaries. These are necessary to form opinions based on our beliefs and to stand by them with confidence. Mental boundaries enable us to have discussions and debates. Porous boundaries will let others devalue your ideas. If someone isn't willing to see things from other people's perspective it might be that their mental boundaries are too rigid!

It's the emotional boundaries that can be more difficult to understand and maintain. Our emotional boundaries keep our feelings apart from the feelings of others. An important aspect of emotional boundaries is not taking responsibility for other people's feelings as you can only control your own. People's emotions shouldn't dictate yours and you shouldn't feel the need to make sacrifices to feed other people's emotional needs.

This may seem a little advanced when you look at your child who is busy chasing peas with a fork or struggling to grip a crayon properly! Of course, we have to understand a child's limitations and their young age but setting healthy boundaries is an essential life skill to have.

WHY BOUNDARIES MATTER

For a happy family with a strong relationship, healthy boundaries are a must. They can guide the family towards the most suitable behaviour while making sure everyone knows their responsibilities. Boundaries you set within the family will help young children to develop their self-control and this will stay with them during their social interactions.

Boundaries should be fair and something that is talked about between family members. They can't come from one person who simply decides the rules because that could cross the boundaries of others. This is especially the case with two-parent families.

Healthy boundaries should never be about power struggles, whether between adults or adults and children because nobody wins a power struggle. If parents start to remind children of who is in charge, it takes away their independence and they don't have the same opportunities to explore their self-control. It often also only leads to anger as well.

That being said, families should have clear safety boundaries that everyone is aware of. And there should be consequences for crossing boundaries or else nobody will respect the limits.

For boundaries to matter and have a positive impact, they also need to be age-appropriate, adapting to the family needs as children grow up. The consequences for overstepping these limits will also need to adapt as they won't be the same for a 3-year-old as they would for a 13-year-old.

Here are some examples of family boundaries as this is the best way to see how much they matter.

- How we talk to each other
- What happens when people get upset
- Going upstairs or outside without supervision
- Screen time
- Who does what household jobs
- When friends can come over

As children become teens, the boundaries will be more about topics like alcohol and drugs. There may also be conversations about money management and expectations within the family. As they get older, it will be more important to listen to your child and see things from their point of view to set different types of boundaries that everyone feels are fair.

LET'S DOUBLE CHECK YOUR BOUNDARIES ARE IN PLACE

Parents need to have their own boundaries in place in order to set the right example but there is another reason why you should check your own boundaries before helping little ones.

There is no need for me to tell you how busy and non-stop parenting is. The idea of putting your own needs before those of your children is just absurd, even selfish. But without boundaries, you run the risk of burnout. Parents can stretch themselves so thin that they are in no physical or emotional state to be able to look after their children to the best of their abilities. It's something that we all do because there is this unspoken myth that parents do whatever it takes for their children.

On the contrary, a parent who knows their limits and ensures their boundaries are respected is one who has enough sleep, eats a healthy diet, has time to exercise and even time for themselves. Happy parents bring up happy children and they also have the energy to take care of their responsibilities.

Setting your own boundaries takes self-awareness, so it's important to have started working on your emotional intelligence and your triggers. Triggers are a good start for knowing your absolute limit. It also takes a little bit of time for you to think about the different types of boundaries and identify yours.

For example, racism and sexism are boundaries that many feel strongly about. As social interactions become more diverse, it's normal that someone might make a comment or ask a question about race that would make you cringe. It might be just because they are ignorant and do so without thinking they could cause offence. However, when a person knowingly makes a sexist or racist joke, that is a boundary that you won't have crossed.

This is why boundaries take a while to identify. There are a number of situations where you might need to re-evaluate your beliefs and values. In some cases, you will feel confident that your boundaries are in place. Other times, you are aware of your boundaries but others aren't, so they need to be communicated.

The next stage is to communicate your boundaries in an assertive way. People need to know that you are serious but in order to take you seriously, you can't communicate your boundaries when you are angry and frustrated. To assertively communicate your boundaries, make eye contact with the person, and have a relaxed posture but sit up straight, looking forward. Speak with a loud, confident tone and a genuine smile. You aren't punishing or telling the other person off, you are just explaining what you are comfortable with.

If we use the same example as before, to respond to a racist joke in the office you could simply say, "I don't find that sort of humour funny." There doesn't have to be a long conversation about it. The same applies at home. To express a behaviour boundary with a child, you should sit down at their level and say "That's not the sort of behaviour we have in our home" and then try to help them resolve their issue.

If an adult continues to cross a boundary, you need to let them know that there will be consequences. In the case of racist and sexist jokes, there will be office policies regarding this (and if there aren't and it's a problem, there should be).

After letting a person know you don't appreciate that kind of humour and they continue to tell these types of jokes, you should let them know that if they continue, you will report them to management. While this might sound petty, you may find that your threat is much appreciated by others who also dislike these types of jokes but don't know how to communicate their own boundaries. We will look at consequences and children in the next section.

Finally, for your own healthy boundaries, be sure to pay attention to others and not cross their limits. If a child doesn't like you colouring in their book, it's only fair to respect it. If a teen has their door closed, you should knock. After all, you would expect the same in return.

HOW TO TEACH YOUR CHILD ABOUT BOUNDARIES

Nobody likes being the "bad parenting cop" and sadly, we all feel that we overuse the word "No" as soon as they start finding their mobility. The problem is that this tiny little word is crucial for them even at such a young age because it's their first introduction to boundaries. You are, in fact, doing your child a favour with these nos because when they begin preschool or primary school, they will have a better understanding of rules.

The trick to get the most out of this powerful word is to use it in the right way, and that is by taking the authoritative style approach. Without going too much into parenting styles, it's generally accepted that there are three main types. You have the authoritarian style, one where rules are black and white and your word is final. Children are often unaware of rules and consequences before they break them, which doesn't seem fair.

The indulgent parent is one whose style is light on rules and consequences and even when there are consequences, they are often negotiated by the child. These parents feel that their children have natural instincts that will guide them around what is right and wrong.

The authoritative style is in between the two extremes. Boundaries are set and talked about. All family members are also aware of the consequences of overstepping boundaries. When a boundary is broken, the parent follows through with the consequence. The most effective parenting style is one where the rules are clear and consistent.

Here are the three parenting styles in action when a child needs to tidy up their toys.

1. Authoritarian: "I told you to tidy up your toys, but you didn't listen so now they are going in the bin!"
2. Indulgent: "Don't worry darling, I will do it if you promise to tidy up next time!"
3. Authoritative: (Before playing) "You can play with your toys but you have to tidy them up after. If you

don't, I will take them away and you won't be able to play with them!"

To be the authoritative parent, following through with the consequence is essential! That being said, there may be some room for negotiation. If you can see they are getting tired or hungry and an emotional outburst is coming your way, you could offer to help, organising the toys so that they still tidy up a fair share. If they refuse, then some toys will have to be taken away.

If you can feel your emotions boiling up while you are attempting to enforce boundaries, step away. This is especially important if your little one needs time to complete their task. The moment you take to step away gives you the chance to calm down as well as them the time to do what needs to be done before the consequence is carried out. Better still, have try the 'Mummy Needs a Minute' activity that you will find later on.

The aim is not to have children feel like they are being punished (though this may require time and a little maturity to understand). This is often seen as punitive parenting where punishment is used to control them through shouting or threatening rather than effective communication. The aim is to discipline children so that they learn through open communication with firmness and love.

Find ways in your daily life to talk about boundaries. Fortunately, there are so many books and stories about emotions that you can use these to bring up boundaries too. Take Goldilocks and the Three Bears. There is a moral to the story—don't enter someone's home without permission. You can use this to talk about how the bear might have felt when Goldilocks broke their chair or finished their food. Little Rabbit Foo Foo is a more direct example of a book about boundaries and consequences.

Empathy is going to help your little one to understand and respect boundaries, especially when it comes to emotions. As we saw in our milestones, by the age of three, children are starting to see when others are upset and even trying to find solutions to help. No, young children aren't going to take in a meaningful conversation about boundaries but you can still talk about how people will feel in different situations and how this might make them feel.

Another thing that might seem a little advanced but is perfectly easy to introduce is perspective and asking children to see things from other people's point of view. First, ask how they would feel in a certain situation, like a friend not wanting to play with them. Then ask them to imagine how their friend would feel in the same situation.

On a similar note, the more you can expose your child to children and adults that are different to them, the more accepting they will become. It's not just about meeting people from different races and cultures. It's about spending time with people who have different backgrounds and physical abilities, with children who share the same interests and with those who have different likes. Children can be aware of how they feel but there is a big leap from this to understanding how other people feel. Diversity shortens that leap.

Getting back to consequences. One of the best ways to help children understand that their actions have repercussions is to allow for natural consequences. These are the effects of their actions where no adult intervention occurs. Let's look at some examples:

- A child refuses to put their coat on. The natural consequence is that they get cold, wet or both.
- If they don't want to do their homework, the natural consequence when you don't force them to do it is that they get in trouble with their teacher.
- If they don't tidy their toys and you don't do it for them, they are going to struggle to find their favourites.

For children to actually learn from this type of discipline, you have to avoid things like "I told you so". This is called piggyback discipline and takes meaning away from the lesson, turning it more into a punishment. Instead, show empathy. If your child got cold and wet recognise this with phrases like "You must be uncomfortable like that" and follow it up with compassion, in this case, suggesting they take a shower or a bath.

Do not use natural consequences if there is any potential for danger or if the consequence can negatively impact those around you. Common sense is needed when deciding if natural consequences are the best way forward.

YOUR CHILD HAS THE RIGHT TO SAY NO— TEACH THEM HOW!

Nothing makes me cringe more when I hear the words "No kiss, no sweets" or similar attempted bribes. It hurts when adults force children to share their food with other children because that's the "nice thing to do". In no world would you share your favourite sandwich with a co-worker unless you wanted to. How would you feel if your boss came and insisted on it?

Children do have their own instincts, their own moods and needs and these should be respected, more so when it comes to physical boundaries. This is often the case with relatives who expect a kiss or a cuddle. If children don't want to give affection or receive it, it's up to the parents to advocate for them. If children feel that these boundaries aren't respected at this age, they won't feel like they are able to express their boundaries when they are older. When they are older, you aren't always going to be there to advocate for them so they absolutely have to learn how to do it while you are there to support them.

There are some books that can show children examples of healthy boundaries in all types of relationships. Some titles you may want to check out are:

- Speak Up
- I Can Say No
- No Means No!
- I Said No!
- Personal Space Invader
- Will Ladybug Hug?
- Miles Is the Boss of His Body

There is the other side of the coin. What happens when Granny comes in expecting a big hug and a kiss and your little one assertively says "No"? You understand why they have put their foot down, but Granny is left looking shocked and feeling unloved.

To overcome this, you can talk to your child about alternatives. Ask your child if they are comfortable with a handshake, a fist pump, a fist pump with a thumbs up, or a wave. Let relatives know what your little one is comfortable with instead of a hug or a kiss. Finally, when a child says "Stop!" or "I don't like it!" it means something is happening that is getting close to their boundary. When you are tickling your little one and they ask you to stop, even though they are laughing, you need to stop. Don't dismiss their boundary and assume you know best. Instead, fill them with that all-important love and security, tell them that you heard them and that you will stop or that you won't do it again.

Let's end this chapter with some games and activities that can help children learn about their boundaries, let others know about them, and how they can get better at respecting boundaries in the home.

GAMES AND ACTIVITIES TO TEACH BOUNDARIES

While there is no harm in using words like boundaries and natural consequences but that doesn't mean that young children are going to understand the concepts. The following games and activities require little preparation but will show children what boundaries.

The Line on the Floor

Take a piece of tape and stick it a line on the floor. Have a piece of paper or card on each side of the line, one saying "Yes" the other saying "No", it doesn't matter if they are too young to read. Begin by showing your child how to play this game. Think of a situation that has a simple boundary, for example, hitting people. Start on the line and say "Playing with my friend", obviously, as a healthy boundary, you would jump to the yes side. "Hitting my friend when I get angry" and you jump to the no side. There is plenty of freedom here so you can create situations that are relevant to your little one.

I Spy Boundaries

This is a great adaptation of the traditional "I Spy". You may have already adapted the game for younger children by choosing colours instead of letters. All you need to do is add boundary to your game, so "I spy with my little eye, a boundary that is brown". Children look around for physical boundaries that are brown (a gate, a door, etc.).

Hula Hoop Hops

The line of the floor game is very black and white and great to get started but life isn't always so cut and dry. Either with hula hoops or drawing circles on the floor, create four circles in a row. From the first circle, you can discuss situations and encourage your child to jump from one hoop to the next depending on how close your sentence gets to their boundary. In the example of hitting, between playing nicely and a physical outburst, situations might include shouting, throwing things, or saying nasty words.

Puppet Hugs

Take two puppets, even if you just make them out of old socks, two cuddly toys or other toys that represent a character. You could give them funny names like Huggy and Huggless. Take in turns to be Huggy while your child is Huggless and vice versa. As you pretend play, create scenarios where Huggy loves to hug and Huggless doesn't. Act out how each one might behave.

Caring for Plants

If you are looking for a way to introduce natural consequences, plants can help you. Have two plants, one you water and care for regularly and one you don't. Talk about what the plant needs and what might happen when these needs aren't met. Make sure your child sees how the neglected plant starts to wilt as a consequence of not caring for it.

The Ice Cream Experiment

This is another idea for natural consequences, especially taking responsibility for things. Ask your child what they think will happen if they don't put the ice-cream away. Leave it out to melt (small pot or individual ice-cream as we don't want to encourage waste). Make sure they see you throwing it away or better, have them throw it away.

Thumbs Up, Thumbs Down

Thumbs up and thumbs down is a teach children that it's okay to say no and is especially good for children who are non-verbal. It's also excellent for any range of topics whether that's talking about how they feel ("Are you tired?") to likes and dislikes, wants, and later on, more complex sentences such as "Would you feel frustrated if…". Children have to give a thumbs up or thumbs down.

Lollipop Stick People

To help children appreciate different cultures and diversity, take some clean lollipops and different skin-coloured card.

Cut outlines of bodies in the card and use different materials for hair, eyes, and clothes. Combining different facial features on different coloured outlines teaches children that everyone is different. Stick them to the lollipop sticks and there you have puppets for role play too.

Mummy Needs a Minute

Naturally, mummy can be changed for any care giver but this is a chance for children to develop empathy, learn coping strategies, and respect boundaries. As parents' we tend to get a build-up of emotions and rather than exploding, we leave the room. Instead of doing this, set a timer and tell your child that you have some big feelings and you need a minute to just sit and be quiet. With their attention on the timer, they will be less likely to interrupt them. Be sure to say thank you after the timer goes up as a way of praising them.

Bonus Activity: Listen and tidy game.

This game isn't necessarily related to boundaries, but often, one of the biggest challenges we have with little people is tidying up. It's frustrating because you know you can do it in 5 minutes, and you are more likely to avoid drama but it's still their responsibility. Rather than doing it for them, take those 5 minutes and turn tidying into a game. You can literally find any way to play while tidying. You can ask them to find all the animals, all the yellow toys, or all the toys from a certain set. Assuming nothing can be broken, you can have children throw toys into the home to improve hand eye coordination, though I only recommend this for children who are likely to get more in the home than out or else there will be extra tidying.

Some people hear the word boundaries and imagine a cold person who wants to keep their distance. Hopefully from this chapter, you have learnt that it is quite the opposite. Boundaries are essential for all family members to ensure that people have the freedom to express their feelings and needs and for others to respect these wishes.

When we focus play on activities that are related to empathy, diversity, perspective and boundaries children start to learn more about rules, consequences, and levels of tolerance. This is the foundations for them to build their emotional intelligence on, learning more about what triggers them before managing emotions.

Even then, there is still a leap from understanding how they feel and them telling you how they are feeling. The following chapter will be jam packed with ways to help little people find their emotion words!

5

"TELL ME HOW YOU REALLY FEEL"

I don't get to watch many films but one that has always made me laugh is Spanglish and a particular scene where the character of Tea Lioni is in the garden interviewing a Mexican housekeeper. Neither of the women understands a word the other is saying and the blank then confused facial expression seems to say it all.

I think it makes me laugh because I have a deeper understanding of communication barriers. Some years ago, when I first moved to the UK, I spoke no English. At the time, it was terrifying, infuriating, and exhausting. Nevertheless, it was an experience that has stayed with me throughout my whole life and it has helped me to appreciate the struggles parents and children have when it comes to communication barriers.

Even though you are "speaking" in the same language, there are daily barriers that can leave you feeling completely lost. Go back to the last tantrum your child had. It doesn't matter what you do or say, there is no possible way to understand what they are feeling because this emotional ball of fury doesn't have the ability to tell you.

But there are two sides to this coin that parents often forget. As much as we are looking at them wondering what is going through their mind, they are probably looking at us wondering the exact same. Again, they just don't have the ability to ask you!

Now, take a moment to think about an argument you had with a partner or a friend. The air was packed with tension and neither of you was about to make an apology. Instead, with no words, one of you reaches over, holds a hand, and gives it a squeeze or rubs an arm. Communicating feelings isn't just about words and this is why there is no need to wait until children can express themselves verbally to start encouraging them to get better at understanding what they are feeling and finding their own way to let you know.

There has been plenty of theory in the previous chapters so here, we are going to look at ideas, games, and activities, many of which can be incorporated into daily life. Remember, as with all of these ideas, they are not set in stone. There are no rules and no way that by playing with your children you will cause them more harm than good. I'm not going to list them by age as each child develops at their own speed.

You can make the activities easier or harder and there will be some ideas as to how.

ARTS AND CRAFTS

Emotion Masks

There are different versions you can create but all will start with paper plates. The first one is to simply take your paper plates and together, draw, colour, or paint different emotions on the plates. You can add lollipop sticks for the children to hold or string to hold masks in place. Once the masks are ready, you can use them to act out stories or events that would cause these feelings.

A different version would be to cut out large eye holes and a mouth hole (the dimensions would have to be different for parent and child. Hold the mask up to your face and make a facial expression. See if your child can guess the emotion. Take turns practicing different expressions. Because the eyes and mouth give away a lot of our feelings, this is a fun way to get them to focus more on these parts of the face.

Make My Face

Again, use a paper plate or a face template on a piece of card. Draw different sets of eyes (with eyebrows), noses (flared nostrils or screwed up), and mouths (smiling, grimacing in pain, surprised). Cut the facial features out and spread them on the table. Make different faces and see if they can find the matching drawings. If your art skills are limited, print images off or take them from magazines.

Story Stones

I love this activity because you can start outdoors exploring. Collect some different stones when you go for a walk. Remember for younger ones, bigger ones will be better as their coordination with a paintbrush might not be as developed. Use acrylic paints to paint different emotions on the stones. Sometimes it helps to have an image that children can try and copy. Once the stones have dried, use them to talk about experiences and/or make up stories that cause the emotions.

Emotions Poster

Ask your child to name as many emotions as they can. On a big piece of card, create separate sections depending on the number of emotions they listed. You may want to add a few extras too. Search through magazines, newspapers, and other material you have at hand to find examples of these emotions. Stick the images in the corresponding sections. You can also add images that cause these feelings. For example, you could add a picture of an adult shouting in the sad section.

Roll a Dice

Use a dice template that is at least A4 in size. If you have a box you could use this instead of making one. I find the larger the box, the more fun children have. On each side of the box, stick or draw an image of an emotion. Roll the dice. Children can name the emotion, copy the facial expression, or talk about how they feel.

An extension of this would be to make two dies, one with images and the other with words. Children can roll both die or you roll one each and see if you can match the image with the word.

Playdough Faces

Much like Make My Face, have a face template and different coloured play dough. You can make facial expressions or use images. See if the children can make the facial expression that they see, talking about which one they think it is. Instead of showing them an image, you can ask them if they can make a surprised face or a tired face.

Matching Facial Expressions

Draw several circles with ears. If you are going to draw hair, make sure each one has the same hairstyle because children may learn to match the hairstyle rather than the facial expression. Draw different emotions on the paper, focusing on the eyes and mouth. Cut out the faces and then cut them in half from ear to ear. See if the children can match the eyes to the mouth to create complete facial expressions. To improve empathy and understanding of diversity, use various skin-coloured paper, again, making sure there is enough variety for them not to just match colours over emotions.

Finger Painting

For younger children, take away the paintbrushes and have some messy fun. Let them use their fingers to paint different faces and feelings. To help young children develop fine motor skills, I like to provide them with a fingerprint template. I have included a very simple example.

SONGS AND WORD GAMES

Wake Up With a Song

Sometimes, children just need a little bit of silly fun so rather than sing one of the more usual songs children love, make up some new ones. Here are some lyrics that you can both start your day too.

- Good morning good morning. How are you today? I'm excited because the sun is shining.
- Wake up sleepy head and tell me how you feel.
- It's Monday and I'm happy because I get to see my friends. How about you?

Next, you just have to add a tune. You can use a tune from popular children's songs or the last song you heard on the radio.

Mix up Your Voice

Certain emotions are expressed with a particular tone of voice. An angry person will speak with a deeper tone. Happiness makes people speak in a higher tone. When you are tired, you may notice less enthusiasm in your tone whereas when you are excited, you might speak faster.

Try mixing up your tone and speed with different facial expressions. For example, you might have an angry expression but speak in a higher tone. Or have a tired look on your face while speaking in a surprised way, emphasising words like "You will *NEVER* believe...".

Mirror, Mirror

A mirror can help children recognise emotions and their own facial expressions as well as learn more about yours. Have your child look into a mirror and say things like "Mirror, mirror in my hand, I can see a grumpy child". Have them make the facial expression.

If You're Happy and You Know It

The traditional song goes "If you're happy and you know it clap your hands" and they clap twice. But you can change the words to absolutely any emotion and create actions to match. I would start with "If you're happy and you know it give me a smile". Here are some more examples.

- If you're tired and you know it have a yawn
- If you're sad and you know it have a cry
- If you're mad and you know it frown your face
- If you're scared and you know it let out a scream

Twinkle Twinkle Emotional Star

Twinkle twinkle has always been a little star but we can once again break out our creativity in two ways. First, the star can be any adjective that can teach children emotional awareness. With the same tune, sing "Twinkle twinkle friendly star...". Another way to change this popular song is to sing the first line as a question to your child. If you can get their name to rhyme, even better. Instead of singing the second line, pause for them to respond. For example "Twinkle twinkle little Sam, how are wonder how you are? If you can't use their name, use my favourite "little one".

I Went to The Emotional Shop and Bought...

I love games that work on multiple skills and this one is a perfect example. The traditional game begins with one person saying, "I went to the shop and I bought..." and they would add an item. The next person has to repeat the opening line, the item the first person bought, and then add their own. We can adapt this game to feeling adjectives.

You can start by saying "I woke up this morning and I felt calm". They would then have to repeat it before thinking of their own word. You both keep going adding words until the person can't remember the full list. I love this activity because as well as thinking of different emotions, children also have to use their listening skills, concentration, and memory.

Happy Finger, Happy Finger

Many parents will have heard "Mummy finger, mummy finger, where are you" they cringe at the thought of repeating the same tune for each family member. Take a pen (non-toxic) and draw little emotional faces on their fingertips. Sing the song as they look for the fingertip that corresponds to your lyrics. You can also do this the other way around, they wiggle an emotional fingertip and you sing the corresponding line.

ORGANISING EMOTIONS

The Mood Meter

In previous books, we have used the emotions thermometer to help children express their emotions. On a large piece of paper or card, draw a thermometer. Use different colours for different emotions, starting with calm/happy at the bottom and working your way up to frustrated/angry. Take photos of all the family members and stick them onto pegs or paper clips. At a time of the day when you are all together, take your pegs/clips and place the photo on the emotional thermometer. Take turns in talking about how you feel and what happened during the day to cause this.

An extension of the emotions thermometer is the mood meter. This quadrant (that you can colour) is a way for children to recognise the relationship between emotions and energy levels. The example we have here is a simplified mood meter. Once your little one sees the relationship, you can add more emotions based on their own emotional experiences.

```
                    |  Scared          Excited
                    |
              Angry |
                    |        Confident
                    |_____
                    |
                    |  Sad
Energy              |
                    |        Pleased
              Tired |
                    |        Calm
                    |
         Depressed  |

                    Happiness  →
```

Starting with depressed, you can see that feeling depressed presents with the least amount of happiness and also comes with the lowest energy levels. You can also see how calm, pleased, confident, and excited are all at the higher end of the happiness scale yet also require different levels of energy.

Photo Matching

This activity gives you the chance to bond by looking at old photos. You can talk to your child about your past experiences and how they made you feel. It's a wonderful way to share memories. While digital is great, nothing beats printed photos in an album. You could even start a new feelings album with photos of them and some of their different experiences. For this, you will need to try and take photos of them as they express their different feelings, even though you might not think of taking a photo mid-tantrum!

Memory Game

You can choose between images only, words only, or images and words. You can hand-make your memory cards or print them off. The good news is that this is a game that can easily be added to. So you can start with four or five emotions and when they get good at uncovering the pairs, create a couple more cards to introduce.

Balloon Matching

This is a slightly different, and often more entertaining, version of the memory game and is ideal when you have leftover balloons from a party! Use a pen to draw faces on the balloons. Imagine you have 12 balloons, this would be enough for six emotions, two balloons for each. You can put the balloons in a big box or spread them around the room. Say an emotion and see if they can find the pairs. The more balloons the merrier!

Feelings Ladder

Draw a ladder on a piece of paper. Create flashcards with different emotions, like the thermometer, starting with calm and increasing the intensity. Begin talking about a happy situation. It can be about them playing with a friend or sibling, or even back to that moment when they finish their last mouthful of vegetables before that savoured piece of chicken. As the story progresses, ask your child to choose the cards and place them on the ladder. You could even look at coping strategies for each emotion they put on the ladder.

Peek-a-Boo Feelings

As both of you can take turns, this game can help both of you get better at reading facial expressions. It will also help children to make more eye contact. Hold a blanket or cloth in front of your face. Make a facial expression and slowly move the blanket down so that they can see more of your face. See how quickly they can guess your emotion.

IDEAS FOR MINDSET

The reasons for these activities go beyond emotional intelligence but they are all part of the package. Generally speaking, we get stuck between extremes, a positive mindset, or a negative one. A fixed mindset or a growth one. It's impossible that children, and adults, will always be positive and focused on personal development. At the same time, we want to encourage children to appreciate, the positive and when they are lacking the confidence to try new things, we want to show them that they are capable of amazing things.

My Heart Map

Draw a big heart, again, you can choose between card or paper. Create sections within the hearts. You could have one section for toys, another for family, one for other people, one for their hobbies, or anything that makes them happy. Depending on their age, they can draw pictures or cut out images they find. Fill each section with pictures of things that make them smile, laugh, feel loved, and happy.

Pop the Bubble

For those who love bubbles, you can use this activity to process emotions or let go of beliefs and negative thoughts that are holding them back. Do this first so that you can show them how the theory works. Explain that as you blow a bubble, you are going to take a deep breath and imagine your harmful thought filling up your lungs. As you breathe out and blow the bubble, the bubble gets filled up with the thought. Pop the bubble to say goodbye to it.

Journalling

This is a more permanent version of the emotion thermometer and can also be adapted for different age groups. On a very basic level, fold several pieces of paper in half. At the bottom of each page, write the day of the week and the date. Have a handful of emotions images ready for them to choose from. Stick their emotion on that day of the week. There could be more than one. Try to talk about what is behind each emotion too.

For older children, you can have feeling words that they can trace over to go with their images and if they are writing, draw a few lines for them to write some words or even sentences.

Super Hero Pose

Despite professionals trying to refute the original findings, time and time again, researchers have linked the power pose or the superhero pose with an increased feeling of power and confidence, even in children. It only takes 120 seconds of posing like a superhero to increase testosterone (the dominance hormone) by around 20 per cent and decrease cortisol (the stress hormone) by around 25 per cent (Kreiss, 2014).

Most of us can imagine a superhero pose and children can probably jump straight into it without much prompting. Nevertheless, double-check that their feet are spread wider than their hips, their hands are resting on their hips, their chest is puffed out and they are looking up.

If you know there is something coming up that is causing them some anxiety, have them stand in the pose and count their breaths up to 10. You may find that a timer will help them stay in the position for longer.

The Kindness Challenge

Helping others can be rewarding for children. It may help to reduce their stress, improve their mood, and strengthen social bonds. It can help them to see the impact of their positive actions, which often encourages them to carry out more. In a world full of corruption, dishonesty, and wrongdoings, it's a gift to bring up a child who prioritises kindness. Sit down with your child and brainstorm some acts of kindness they can do. Here are some ideas.

- Clean up a mess that wasn't theirs
- Do a chore without being asked
- Hold the door open for someone
- Draw a picture for a friend
- Donate old clothes and toys to those in need
- Say hello/good morning/good afternoon to people
- Write a thank you note to the postman/ rubbish collectors
- Invite a lonely child to play with them
- Say something nice to their friend or family member (pay them a compliment)
- Bake cupcakes and take them to a residential home

Be sure to talk about their acts of kindness and how they made other people feel. This is also an important moment to tell your little one how proud you are of them.

Famous Fails

We often try to protect our children from failure, like it's some contagious disease but the truth is, we can learn a lot more from mistakes than we can from our successes, and the same can be said for children. In order to show children just how much we can learn from mistakes, we can retell stories of well-known people and their rise from rock bottom.

A quick Google search for 'famous failures' and you will get dozens of examples, one that your child can relate to. Considering how famous Mickey Mouse is, I tend to use Walt Disney as an example.

Walt Disney had a horrible, cruel father, and he left home when he was young to join the army and fight in the war. After the war, he started an animation company but it was too expensive. He lost all his money and was so poor he had to eat dog food. he created Oswald the Lucky Rabbit but somebody stole his idea. He created Mickey Mouse but was rejected 300 times before Mickey became a success. Walt Disney was even fired from one of his first jobs because he wasn't creative enough.

Telling children stories like that can encourage them to stick at things and that it's normal to find some things challenging, but perseverance leads to amazing outcomes.

BURNING OFF PENT UP EMOTIONS

Charades

The slight twist on this classic game is that on pieces of paper, you have dozens of different emotions and feelings. Each person playing takes a turn to take a piece of paper and acts out the word on the paper. The person who guesses gets to take the next turn. That being said, you may prefer to let everyone have a go regardless of who guesses the answer.

Emotions Obstacle Course

This will require a little bit of set up but you can use everyday objects that you can find around the home. For example, sofa cushions can become hopping stones, hula hoops can be hung in the doorway, and air dryers for clothes as tunnels. Make each activity an emotion. Call out an emotion and watch them carry out the activity. To encourage them to pay more attention, you can give them a series of emotions and check that they get the order of the activities correct.

How Do You Feel Little Animal

Take advantage of the fresh air and time away from devices with a walk. As you are on your walk, see how many animals you can find and how those animals might be feeling. This is great because you have the opportunity to show children that it's okay to have different opinions. Imagine you see a bird in the sky. You can ask your child how they think the bird might be feeling.

They could come up with ideas like free and excited. In return, you can reply, with "Wow, they are good answers. I think the bird is bored. It's just flying around in circles doing nothing". Children have such wonderful imaginations, they might come back and tell you that the bird is hungry and looking for food.

Emotions Bowling

Start saving your plastic bottles, preferably the same size and typically ten bottles. We want each of the bottles to have an emotion. You can draw faces at stick them on the bottles, use your balloon faces, or paper plate faces. Add a little rice or water to the bottles to weigh them slightly. Children have to name the emotions of the pins they knock down.

Feelings Treasure Hunt

There is plenty of room for creativity and personalisation in this game but you will need to plan ahead a little bit in order to have your clues ready. Here are some examples of clues you could set up.

- I'm your favourite toy that makes you happy
- This is the place where you go to when you feel tired
- I am a room in the house to go when I'm hungry
- When (insert family member) is angry, they go here
- I am a donkey who is always depressed (or other characters they have)

Have a small prize at the end of the treasure hunt as a reward for their efforts.

USING TECHNOLOGY

There is a difference between placing children in front of the TV for a few hours and using technology as a learning tool. In today's digital world, it's impossible to escape technology, and considering its use in the future, there are benefits for children to learn early. In this section, we will look at a few ideas to get the most out of devices.

Make a Video

While you are playing games like Mirror Mirror or singing the songs we saw above, make videos that you can later watch together making different observations. You can also make a video of the two of you or with other family members just messing around with funny faces.

Watch Appropriate Videos

YouTube has a ton of videos that are age-appropriate and teaches children more about their different feelings. That being said, you can also use any video as a learning tool. Much like books, it's a case of pausing the video to ask your child how they think the characters are feeling.

Apps to Teach Emotions

Here are some apps and games you might want to explore with your little ones. Once more, it's best that you play with your children rather than just leave them to play so that they can get the most out of the experience.

- Moody Monster Manor
- The Feelings Book App
- Positive Penguins
- My Peekaville
- Touch and Learn
- Daniel Tiger Grr-ific Feelings
- Hopster Saturday Club
- Bouncy the People Trainer

These are only a small sample of possibilities. Pop onto your app store and type in "feelings and emotions for children" and you will have a wider range of apps.

After all of these games and activities, you might be wondering how you are going to find enough feelings to not get stuck with happy, sad, and angry. Below, you will find a handy word bank. Feel free to print this word bank and keep it handy. The top box has our basic emotions. Once they have mastered them, you can start working on the emotions in the box below. Just remember your little one's limitations. Please don't expect a 3-year-old to be able to identify and express all of these words!

Happy, Sad, Scared, Excited, Grumpy, Angry, Surprised
Bored, Brave, Calm, Cheerful, Confused, Curious, Disappointed, Embarrassed, Excited, Fantastic, Friendly, Frustrated, Generous, Grateful, Guilty, Ignored, Impatient, Important, Interested, Jealous, Lonely, Loving, Overwhelmed, Peaceful, Proud, Relaxed, Relieved, Safe, Satisfied, Shy, Silly, Stubborn, Surprised, Tense, Uncomfortable, Worried

There is one thing I catch myself repeating often is that you don't need any expensive equipment and you don't need long sessions with children to notice a difference in their emotional awareness. It's true that some of the activities that need a little planning are better off as weekend activities, but the majority are perfect for five-minute fillers!

In this chapter, we started to learn how facial expressions are essential for expressing emotions. It's not only the face that can tell us how our little one is feeling. The next step is to discover body language and the more subtle language of emotions.

6

LET'S TALK ABOUT BODY LANGUAGE

Body language is a very powerful tool. We had body language before we had speech, and apparently, 80% of what you understand in a conversation is read through the body, not the words."

— *DEBORAH BULL*

Different experts have come up with their own percentages but the general understanding is that 55 per cent of communication is body language and 38 per cent is voice behaviour (tone, fillers, volume). That leaves us with only 7 percent of communication coming from the words we speak. This is incredibly helpful when it comes to watching our little ones and gaining a better reading of how they are feeling, especially when they aren't sure how to get their emotions across.

Before digging into how to read body language, there is one very important thing that cannot be forgotten. Some children will have difficulties with their own body language as well as reading that of others. Firstly, body language is a skill that needs to be practiced. Secondly, some conditions will impact a child's body language. Those with ADHD may be more restless than others and we can see this with their gestures. Children on the autism spectrum often have difficulties making eye contact.

This doesn't mean that if your child doesn't make eye contact that they are on the autism spectrum. Like milestones, if you notice something about your child's body language and it raises a red flag, it's something to discuss with your doctor before panicking.

WHAT IS BODY LANGUAGE?

Body language is all of the non-verbal cues we give as we communicate. It includes our facial expressions, gestures with our arms, hands, and legs, posture, and also our verbal behaviour. Verbal behaviour covers the way we raise our tone and volume when we are happy or excited, or when we speak slower when we are less enthusiastic. Fillers are sounds we make such as "umm" and "ohh".

Combined, all of these elements can tell us more about how a person is feeling, and more often than not, body language will be more honest than the words someone is saying. This, in turn, enables communication to be better, with more trust and stronger bonds. When looking at a child who seems to be having a tantrum, you may think that they are angry or frustrated. But by looking closer at their body language, you may spot signs of fear in their eyes or anxiety in the way to try to self-soothe. These signs can help you respond in a way that your child needs!

FOCUS ON THE FACIAL EXPRESSIONS

Facial expressions can be classified into macro expressions and micro expressions. Macro expressions are our normal facial expressions lasting anywhere from ½ a second to 4 seconds. Micro expressions are literally a flash at less than ½ a second. This is why micro expressions are often missed in social situations. It may surprise you to know that children with ADHD are highly sensitive to micro expressions and this is why they can seem quick to form opinions. What makes micro expressions so important is that they are involuntary, which means we can't control them!

The eyes really do give away so much of what we are feeling and are often one of the easier parts of the face to read. The right amount of eye contact shows interest, a lack of eye contact could mean a person is shy, anxious, or disengaged. Eye contact that lasts for too long could be a sign of dominance. Eyes that dart all over the place or quickly break contact may indicate someone isn't being truthful. Excessive blinking is another sign that the person is not comfortable.

Along with the eyes, you need to look at what's going on with the eyebrows. Raised eyebrows with wrinkles on the forehead show surprise or disbelief. When the eyebrows are knitted together, it can mean the person is angry or it could just be that they are confused.

The nose doesn't give away too much but that's not to say it should be ignored. Flared nostrils point to an angry person. This is a fight, flight, or freeze response allowing the body to take in more oxygen. A scrunched-up nose suggests disgust (think of the most disgusting food you can imagine and see what happens to your nose. The stress caused by telling lies causes the capillaries in our noses to expand ever so slightly. This is why many people itch their noses when being dishonest.

For the mouth, the first place I like to start is by recognising a genuine smile. The biggest clue to spot a genuine smile is to look for the crow's feet around the eyes. The absence of crow's feet might imply a person is faking their happiness or they are being sarcastic. The extent to which the corners of the lips are turned up, along with the crow's feet can indicate the level of happiness. The same can be said for the level of sadness when the corners of the lips are turned down.

If someone purses their lips and you can see the tension, it's often with a sense of distaste or disapproval. Interestingly, babies as young as 4 weeks old can purse their lips. Lip biting is a sign of nerves, worry, or anxiety. When people attempt to cover their mouths it's often because they are trying to hide something or they want to prevent themselves from saying something.

WHAT YOUR CHILD'S GESTURES MEAN

Starting with the hands, a clenched fist often points to frustration or anger whereas open palms that are facing upward suggest a person is feeling comfortable. Hand tapping and even foot tapping could mean a person is bored or feeling restless. Hiding of the hands, like covering the mouth might be a sign that a person is holding back or trying to hide their feelings.

We have often been told that crossed arms and crossed legs are signs of a person being closed off and distant. It's important to put this into context because it's not always the case. A young child may cross their arms in frustration and it might simply mean that they are cold.

It's the open and closed non-verbal cues to look out for when observing someone's posture. Instead of just looking for crossed arms, look for other signs that show a person's possible unfriendliness or anxiety. These include a lowered head, scrunched-over shoulders, and crossed legs. On the other hand, an open posture is one where a person is sitting up straight, hands are visible and the chest is almost puffed out. This suggests the person is feeling confident and engaged.

A really good sign to look out for in children is the flapping of arms. This is another instinctual reaction to the fight, flight, or freeze response and they are trying to get away from the situation. The situation could be causing them pain or stress. Other signs that a child is uncomfortable is that they might tug at your arm or at a piece of clothing. They may seem a little clingier than usual, burying their head in your legs or lap.

Finally, you can tell a lot by the distance between people, also known as proxemics. There are four levels of personal space that indicate how comfortable a person is feeling and the type of relationship the two people have.

The intimate distance is from 6 to 8 inches and there is more touching and hugging. This close proximity is often a safe zone for people in closer relationships. When you notice people with a distance of 1.5 to 4 feet, it's most likely because they are friends or family members. The closer they are, the stronger the tie. From 4 to 12 feet, we have our social distance and it's typical between people you know but not that well, an acquaintance or co-worker. Anything over 12 feet and we are looking at a public distance, for example, a teacher in front of their class.

It's worth remembering that proxemics vary from culture to culture. In the south of Europe, people tend to feel more comfortable being closer but in northern countries, the same closeness could be seen as an invasion of personal space.

To take advantage of proxemics, look at the personal space between your little one and their teacher on the first day of preschool or school. Compare this with the personal space between the two after a few weeks. As your little one becomes more confident around their teacher, you can expect to see the distance between them close.

HOW DO PEOPLE USE BODY LANGUAGE TO EXPRESS DIFFERENT EMOTIONS?

A little fun fact for you, it was Charles Darwin who originally believed that there were universal emotions, those that aren't impacted by culture. In the late 20th century Dr Paul Ekman, one of the foremost specialists in the study of emotions and facial expressions, tried to prove Darwin's theory wrong. Ironically, Ekman's social experiment proved Darwin's theory to be correct. Here are some tips on reading these universal emotions.

Happiness

In the eyes, you will see crow's feet and a hint of eyes squinting. The cheeks will be raised and this shows lines from the nose to toward the corners of the lips, which will be pointing upward. The mouth might be open and in some cases, the teeth will be showing.

Sadness

A lot of sadness is seen in the eyebrows. They will be lower and pulled together but the inner corners of the eyebrows are pointing upward. This is something that is hard to fake. The eyelids are quite loose, and the corners of the lips point down.

Anger

The eyebrows are pulled down while the eyelids are raised. You might see more whites in the eyes and there will be wrinkles across the forehead. Nostrils could be flared and the lips are tight. This tension can be seen in the jaw too. The corners of the mouth might be turned down. Some children grind their teeth when they are angry.

Fear

Eyebrows are once again raised, pulled together, and with wrinkles across the forehead. You may also see more whites in the eyes. The difference is that the upper eyelids will be raised while the lower eyelids appear tense. The mouth will be stretched, pulled back, and the lips often open.

Surprise

The eyebrows are raised but the distinct difference is that the wrinkles on the forehead appear horizontally instead of vertically with the previous emotions. Eyes will be wide open with the eyelids pulled up. Pupils are likely to be dilated. The jaw drops, leaving the mouth loosely open.

Disgust

The eyebrows are pulled down and the eyes would appear narrow. The upper lip is raised but the lips remain loose. The cheeks are often raised too. It's the wrinkled nose that gives disgust away. This is an instinctual reaction to make nostrils smaller so that less smell or fumes can be taken in.

Contempt

The eyes are neutral, possibly black or unengaged but it's normal to see one raised eyebrow. One side of the mouth is pulled back with the same corner of the lips slightly raised. The head could be tilted back just enough to give the impression that they are looking down their nose at you. The more obvious the movements, the greater the level of contempt.

10 THINGS TO TEACH YOUR CHILD ABOUT BODY LANGUAGE

Now that we understand how important body language is in communication, it makes sense that we take opportunities to teach children about their non-verbal cues. These life skills can be taught to children as soon as they show signs of understanding instructions, typically around the age of 2. Most of this learning will be in the form of games and activities, but there are also some things we can explain to children to gain more understanding.

1. All of our body language has meaning. The way you move your hands or use your eyes can tell other people how you are feeling. We can practice our body language and you can learn a lot from watching us and your friends.
2. Your brain controls your movements and your words but it also controls your facial expressions and the smaller gestures you make with your hands, arms, and legs. We have to be careful about the words we use but also, the body language we use.
3. (while watching a baby crying/laughing). We can tell how the baby feels when they laugh or cry. I can tell when you are angry when you stomp your feet and I can tell when you are excited because you wave your arms around.
4. Your movements are more accurate and honest than the words you speak. That's because there are some movements that we can't control. Many times, I know how you feel before you use your words.
5. If you can pay attention to your friends and look for signs that they are sad, angry, or anxious, you will be able to have more fun with them. It makes it easier to know when they need help or when they need comfort.

6. Your body language can hurt just as much as your words can. When you frown your face, cross your arms, and huff at me, it can hurt as much as when you shout at me because you are mad.
7. You can also use your body language to show me that you care and you don't need to use any words. You can blow me a kiss, give me a hug, or hold my hand and I know you love me. Just like body language can hurt people, it can also make them very happy.
8. If you want something, I can often tell what it is that you want by your body language. If you are nervous, your eyes move around a lot. If you want to leave, your feet change direction and point towards the door.
9. Not everybody likes to be as physically close to other people. I love your hugs and when you sit close to me but you have to understand that some people prefer more space. You don't need to be upset about this, but you can help them by respecting their space.
10. If your body tells you that your brain or your body doesn't feel safe or comfortable, please let me know. You can tell me what makes you feel this way and I will understand. Or, we can try to work out together what is upsetting you.

ACTIVITIES TO HELP WITH BODY LANGUAGE

Simon Says

To put a twist on the traditional game, the person who gives the instructions should focus on actions that require body language. Some instructions can include.

- Show me your angry hands
- Pull a surprised face
- Make your feet look bored
- Be cold/hot
- Look shy
- Stare at me

Blinking Baddies

This is a game that is better with more people, so you can save it for when your child has friends over. The original game uses winking but if they can't wink yet, blinking is easier. Choose one of the children to be the "baddie" and another to be the detective before having them sit in a circle. The baddie has to blink at other children in the group and they slump to the floor. The detective has to decide which child is the baddie before all the children are slumped on the floor.

Mimes

Here, we have an extension and a slightly more challenging version of charades. While charades is a game of guessing the emotions, you can extend miming for children to guess a whole scenario. With charades, most of the focus will be on their facial expressions but because they have to mime a situation, they will need to use more body language. On a piece of paper, write some of these possible scenarios.

- Grandma has given you a new phone for your birthday
- You have to tidy your bedroom and make your bed
- Your friend wants you to sleep at their house and you need to ask your parents
- You have a test at school tomorrow
- You are not allowed to watch TV all afternoon

Nod Your Needs

We are used to saying things like "Can you pass me the…" and supporting this by pointing a finger at the object. However, if you take away the words and your finger, you now have to rely on nodding at an object you want. Ask your child to put some toys on the floor. To start off a bit easier, they can be lined up in a row. Once that becomes easy, spread them out, and then you can even make it harder by bringing the toys closer. Take turns in nodding at objects to see if they can guess what you want.

Opposites Game

I love this game to teach children how confusing communication is when words and body language don't match. You may have tried to rub circles on your stomach while you pat your head. The opposites game is similar. You can have children nod their heads in agreement when they want to say no. You can have them say something exciting but have their arms crossed. This chapter will have given you plenty of contradicting examples.

Spot the Emotion

Your child will love to run around at the park with their friends but there are often moments when they come and sit next to you for a drink, a hug, or to tell you something. Take this opportunity to ask them to look at their friends and see if they can spot body language and the various meanings. Naturally, for them to recognise the meaning behind gestures, they will need to be taught some of the most important gestures.

There are a lot of "whens", "ifs", and "maybes" in this chapter on body language and this is because everyone is different, regardless of age. After the universal signs, it's crucial that you pay close attention to your child to understand their baseline. A baseline is what is considered typical for them.

For example, they might fiddle with their hair, not as a way of self-soothing but just because they like it. They might blink more than other children, so you wouldn't assume the worse because they are blinking a lot. When you are aware of the baseline, you will be able to recognise the signs that something is off with them. When one of mine was little, they used to get angry any time they hurt themselves. You would expect them to want a hug or a kiss but instead, they wanted to be left alone. For an accurate understanding, it's necessary not to compare your child's body language with others, but to decipher what is typical for them.

The good news about learning your child's non-verbal cues is that it will be of significant help when it comes to understanding what is going on with their big feelings. In the next chapter, we will look at coping strategies for when it feels like their world is coming apart.

FREE GOODWILL

He who said money can't buy happiness hasn't given enough away. By Anonymous

People who help others with zero expectations experience higher level of fulfillment, live longer and make more money.

I want to create an opportunity to deliver this value to you during your reading or listening experience. In order to do so I have one simple ask, would you help someone you have never met, it wouldn't cost you any money and you'll never get credit for it?

If so then I have a request on behalf of someone you do not know and likely never will meet.

They are just like you or like you were a few months/years ago, less experienced and full of desire to help their child, seeking information but unsure where to look. This is where you come in.

The only way for us at Kids SLT Publishing to accomplish our mission of helping parents this first by reaching them, and most people do in fact judge a book by its cover and its reviews.

If you have found this book valuable and helpful thus far, would you please take a moment right now and leave an honest review of the book and its contents. It will cost you zero pounds/dollars and takes less than 60 seconds.

- Your review will help those parents who are looking for advice and strategies to help their child.
- Your review will help another child reach their potential
- Your review will help another parent feel better that they have found a helpful resource
- Your review will help a parent feel less anxious and more confident in their abilities with the help of this book.
- Your review will help one more life change for the better

To do this, all you have to do is, and it only takes less than 60 seconds, is to leave a review. If you are on audible click the three dots and choose 'review'.

If you are reading a paperback please search for this book on Amazon, click on the book, scroll down the page, and click on 'leave customer review'. If you don't have time to write a review, you can leave star rating only but even a sentence would be extremely valuable.

You can also scan the QR code or visit the link below to leave a quick review!

https://www.amazon.co.uk/dp/B0BZRXB3PX?geniuslink=true

If you introduce something valuable to someone, they will associate that value with you. If you would like goodwill directed from another parent then send this book their way

Thank you from the bottom of our heart, and now back to your regular programming!

7

HELPING YOUR CHILD COPE WITH BIG FEELINGS

"When you react, you let others control you. When you respond, you are in control."

— BOHDI SANDERS

It's a thought-provoking quote from Bohdi Sanders and it sounds obvious, but few people will stop to think about whether they are a reactor or a responder. Each day, we are faced with an endless number of situations where we can either react or respond, and they aren't just caused by our triggers.

When faced with challenges, there are normally two possible outcomes. We can resist, deny, fight back, oppose, or shift the blame. This form of reacting shifts responsibility from ourselves onto others. This inevitably ends in the situation getting worse. Imagine your child refuses to get dressed and you huff and puff, complain that you have to do everything in the house, and struggle with them as they wiggle arms into the wrong holes.

On the other hand, we have responders. Those people who are faced with the same situation but instead of feeling like the world is fighting against them, will think about the best possible outcome, the solution to get there, and take action.

Again, whether it's a trigger or not, reactors tend to suffer from massive emotional outbursts. I don't use the word suffer lightly. A reactor feels like the person who is not in control of their feelings is doing it on purpose and that they are actually suffering more. A responder appreciates that emotional outbursts are enjoyed by neither party, in fact, they are physically and emotionally exhausting.

WHAT DOES EMOTIONAL DYSREGULATION LOOK LIKE?

When looking at typical children, once you get past the terrible twos and those frequent tantrums, children around the ages of 3 and 4 start to learn how to control their emotions better. It will be far from perfect, but they are beginning to develop their coping skills. This is called self-regulation, the ability to manage emotions and behaviour according to certain situations.

When children aren't able to develop this skill, it is called emotional dysregulation. There are several reasons why emotional dysregulation occurs. In some cases, it can be caused when a baby is unable to soothe themself. These babies become extremely upset or distressed during relatively simple tasks like dressing them. As they get older, the ability to regulate emotions remains difficult.

In other cases, emotional dysregulation is personality based or caused by their environment. Sometimes, a parent can try so hard to comfort their child that the child struggles with self-discipline in relation to emotions. Here are some other reasons and conditions where emotional dysregulation may arise.

- Childhood trauma
- Neglect
- Chronic low levels of invalidation
- ADHD
- ASD
- Social anxiety
- Frontal lobe disorder or damage

Let's get one thing very clear. In no way am I suggesting that you neglect your child or that you have caused any type of brain injury. A frequent misconception is that childhood trauma is related to some form of abuse. But this is far from the truth. Childhood trauma can include anything from the death of a loved one to war and displacement. For those who have adopted children, you may never know their full history, and therefore dwelling on what might be the cause is less productive than taking steps to help!

What's important now is to focus on teaching children how to regulate these massive feelings that lead them to be mini reactors so that they grow up to be responders.

UNDERSTANDING THE POLYVAGAL THEORY AND 7 ACTIVITIES TO PRACTICE IT

A quick biology lesson to get us started! Our bodies have a central nervous system which is made up of the brain, the spine, and the autonomic nervous system. The autonomic nervous system controls the involuntary systems in our body like breathing and digestion. Within the autonomic nervous system, we have the sympathetic nervous system (SNS), the parasympathetic nervous system (PNS), and the enteric nervous system.

The SNS is what controls our fight or flight response while the PNS is also known as 'rest and digest' mode. The Enteric nervous system controls the gastrointestinal tract and digestion. This is why you may feel sick when you are nervous or have butterflies in your stomach. What links all of these systems together is the vagus nerve, the 10th cranial nerve. It begins in the brain, and passes the ear and vocal cords before branching off to different organs and systems such as the heart, lungs, kidneys, liver, gall bladder, and gut.

Professor Stephen Porges who proposed the polyvagal theory believes that humans automatically and subconsciously scan environments for potential danger. This process is called neuroception and relies on the senses detecting different information and feeding it back to the brain. The body then responds in one of three ways, fight, flight, or freeze. The body will naturally use the most evolved stress response but if that doesn't work, it will rely on a more primitive response.

When all is well as we are comfortable in our surroundings, the PNS is engaged. Heart rate and breathing are normal and our bodies are able to perform all the necessary functions. When neuroception detects danger, the SNS kicks in, heart rate and breathing increase, pupils dilate, and even our hearing becomes fine-tuned to pick up on danger. A rush of adrenaline prepares the body for fight or flight.

Porges proposed that when this doesn't work, the vagus nerve goes back to its most primitive form, freeze! This is a unique response that we share only with reptiles and it is seen when they 'play dead'. Essentially, within the PNS, the vagal nerve reduces the body's automatic abilities to function.

While slightly unrelated, I feel it's crucial to mention one point in the hope that we can all become a little more empathetic. When a person experiences a crime or other type of trauma, one of the first things think (or worse say) is why didn't they run, or why didn't they fight? Because in that moment, their body had completely taken over, and to freeze was the only thing that their survival instincts were telling them to do!

Bringing the polyvagal theory back to children, there are two things to point out. Neuroception involves scanning for danger and this includes perceived danger. You might bump into a friend and know there is no harm, but your little one's senses may not be telling them the same. It's easy for us to say "It's nothing to be scared off" but every part of their body could be telling them the opposite—and they can't control this.

Secondly, in freeze mode, people can become inanimate, as if there are no signs of life. When a child doesn't respond to you, it's not because they don't want to or that they aren't listening. They physically can't until their SNS and PNS return to their normal states.

Because of the role of the vagus nerve within the autonomic nervous system, a marvellous tool to help children (and adults) when these big emotions become too much is to stimulate the vagus nerve. By stimulating the vagus nerve, we can encourage the body to return to its 'rest and digest' mode more quickly. The following activities are simple enough for most ages.

Deep breathing

I always feel like deep breathing is old and recycled advice, but it has been proven to calm people down over and over again. Controlling your breathing allows the heart rate to slow down and stress hormones to decrease. You will hear many deep breathing techniques but for now, keep it simple. One of the most commonly used techniques is the 4-7-8 exercise where you inhale for 4 seconds, hold your breath for 7 seconds, and exhale for 8 seconds. The calming effect is still achieved as long as you make sure you exhale for longer than you inhale.

Closed exhalation

Start by breathing normally and have your child copy you. Close your mouth and then pinch your nose enough so that a tiny amount of air can escape. Exhale for 25 to 20 seconds. It's important not to force the exhalation but you will notice extra pressure in the chest and this is what stimulates the vagus nerve.

Cold water

This sounds like an old wives' tale but science has been able to prove that splashing cold water on your face or immersing your face in cold water can reduce stress. It can lower your heart rate and encourage the release of happy hormones in the brain.

Using vocals

As the vagus nerve runs close to the vocal cords, a quick and easy way to stimulate it is to hum, sing, or gargle. In yoga, it's common to chant mantras to benefit from these vibrations but that's not necessary as it can be any tune. As well as having your little ones sing their favourite tune, try teaching them how to hum it as well.

Happy memories

This may require a little practice and for children, a little help from you. Thinking about past happy memories also releases happy hormones in the brain. That being said, you know how hard it is to think about something positive when you are overwhelmed by stress. For your child, talk them through the experience. For example, "remember when we went to the swimming pool, and you went down the big slide…".

Playful distractions

As adults, we forget the importance of play but playing stimulates our response to social engagement, even tapping into the inner child in all of us. All it may take is to make sure you are in your child's line of sight and start to play with some of the toys they love. Don't force them or nag them to play with you, just let them know you are they when they are ready.

Change the environment

Because the senses are working overtime, all you (or your child) might need is a change of environment so that the neuroreceptors are picking up on new messages. Think about colours, smells, sounds, and textures that make you and your little one feel safe. It could be simple things like turning down the brightness of a light, offering them their favourite soft toy, or lighting an aromatherapy candle.

Traffic Light Emotions

You can use three colours and a traffic light system to let your children express their levels of fear and anxiety and this way, help them to calm down before they feel like they are unsafe or out of control. Imagine giving your child three laminated flashcards on a keyring. They don't have to be large and they don't need words or images. One is green, the other orange, and the third red. Now imagine going into a situation where you know your child may have difficulties. They would start off holding the green card but as their body starts to respond and the levels of discomfort increase, they switch to the orange card. This is a sign for you to start paying more attention, offering words of comfort and reassurance. By paying more attention to their body language, we can see when they are about to switch to the red card and pull them out of the situation before an outburst.

WHAT PARENTS CAN DO TO HELP CHILDREN WITH SELF-REGULATION

We have previously seen how understanding triggers is one of the first steps to self-regulation. In time, children will become more aware of what triggers them and how to cope with the situation. We have also discovered that rather than minimising or ignoring a child's feelings, we should be validating them, reassuring them that it is okay to feel the way they do. Finally, we have looked at activities that can help children label their emotions. However, I wanted to take this opportunity to introduce primary and secondary emotions.

A child might experience an emotion but are unaware that there was a primary emotion that comes first. It's also true that most of us experience mixed emotions and that there are in fact primary, secondary, and tertiary emotions. You can do a quick search for 'Emotion Wheels' and there will be various examples from different researchers. However, I have created a very simple version (combining some of the secondary and tertiary emotions) to help little people get a better understanding of what they are actually feeling. Feel free to print my wheel and colour it in or add emotions that you see fit for your child.

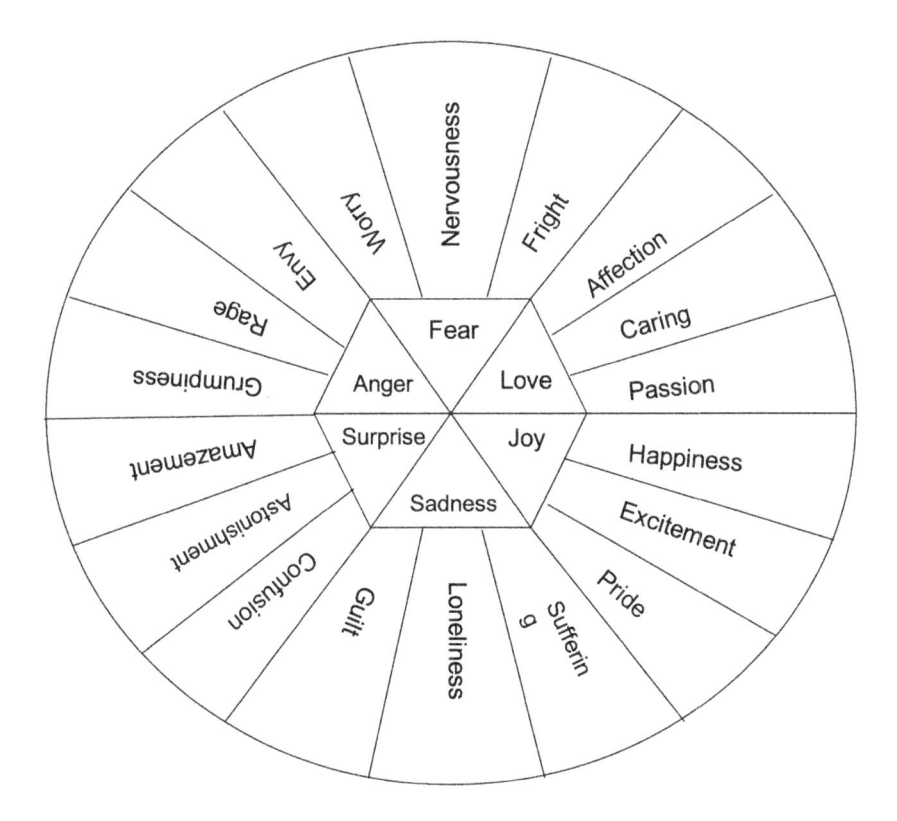

Remember, this is my version. You may want to change, for example, envy to jealousy or shame to guilt. In your home, you might not use grumpy as much, but you prefer annoyed or grouchy. There are dozens of "professional wheels" you can use and they are all great, but whenever possible, I try to make this more personal and therefore relevant.

You can also use your emotions wheel to teach children that emotions come and go. In a particular moment, they might feel huge amounts of rage which after a moment, becomes anger, and then sadness before they understand more about the situation and the solution. The wheel can be a visual guide for them to get from one emotion to another.

Self-regulation is a skill that takes time to develop and while it is being developed, parents can help by being a scaffolding or support for their children. Now, there is a significant difference between being supportive and hovering. When children have to carry out a task that causes them frustration, it's common for parents to sit close by, perhaps interrupt to check that things are going okay. What this can actually do is cause children to relate their frustration to the behaviour of their parents.

Supporting children can be about setting a timer so you both know when a break is coming up. It could be telling your child that you will be back in 5 minutes to see how they are getting on (and taking advantage of those 5 minutes to get a job or two done). When you go back to see how they are doing, you can offer them praise for their progress and ask if they would like some help if they are stuck.

Like all skills, you are going to want to start with small steps. If you wanted to learn how to ride a horse or play an instrument, you wouldn't sign yourself up for any type of competition before practicing. Self-regulation is the same. Allow children to practice by breaking troublesome situations down into smaller, achievable steps. If shopping is a particular challenge for them, you would start by making sure you plan a trip to the supermarket when they aren't tired or hungry. Then makes sure it's a short trip for just the basics. Give them the list with just a few things so they can see that it's not a full-on shopping trip. Gradually build up on this, praising them for each successful shop.

Finally, self-regulation can't be rushed through. It's all well and good praising the good but it's unreasonable to expect children to master this skill straight away. Self-reflection is a crucial part of the learning process and parents needn't shy away from talking about what could have gone better. This is how children learn for the next time.

Use the sandwich technique to provide children with constructive criticism. First let them know something they did well, then something that could be improved, and then end on another thing that they achieved.

To further support this, you can strengthen your example-setting skills by talking to your child about your own efforts towards emotional regulation, the things you did well, and areas that could be improved. Even try asking for feedback from them, it's an eye-opening experience!

13 MINDFUL EXERCISES FOR CHILDREN

Mindfulness is often considered the latest buzzword but there is plenty of evidence to support the benefits of this practice for both adults and children. Mindfulness is about focusing on breathing while letting emotions come and go while focusing on the senses and the present moment. It helps people to stop worrying about the past and the future and allows them to calm down in the moment.

Mindfulness is particularly helpful for children with ADHD, anxiety, autism, or those who struggle with emotional regulation unrelated to specific disorders. One study looked at the brain activity of children as they watched a distressing video. Some children counted backward as a way of distraction, others used simple forms of meditation. Those using meditation showed decreased activity in the area of the brain that is associated with negative thinking, rumination, and mind-wandering (Marusak, 2022).

Let's get straight into some mindfulness activities that can benefit all the family!

Body scan

Lie down with your child and talk them through the process. You may have to do this a few times until they can do it by themselves. Begin by focusing on your breathing, counting in sets of 5 if it helps you calm down. When you are feeling calm, focus your attention on one part of the body, and spend a few minutes mentally scanning the area noticing any feelings there might be, tingling, tension, aches, or pains without trying to work out why or what to do about it. Just notice it. Then move on to the next part of the body. To help keep focus, it's easier to start at the feet and work your way up the body.

Use your senses

This is a lovely activity to engage the senses and focus only on the present. You can start at a very basic level, asking your child to name one thing they can see, smell, taste, touch, and hear. To make the activity longer, or more challenging, you can increase the number of things they have to name (this may depend on where you are and what you are doing). For example, they can name 5 things they can see, 4 things they can hear, 3 things they can taste, 2 things they can touch, and 1 thing they can taste.

Mindful eating

If you struggle to get your child to eat in a reasonable amount of time, mindful eating may seem counterproductive. On the contrary, if a child takes too long to eat, it's most likely that they are distracted. Mindful eating encourages people to engage all of their senses when eating instead of just wolfing down their food. You can focus on the taste, the texture, the smell, and even the colour of each mouthful.

Legs up the wall

The yoga position legs up the wall is a restorative position, so it is meant to slow the body and mind down. When the legs are elevated, the heart doesn't have to work as hard. In turn, the heart rate slows down. Have your little one lay on the floor and shift their bum towards the wall. Stretch their legs up to the ceiling and rest them against the wall. Try to encourage them to stay there for 5 minutes. Of course, this will be easier if you do it with them.

Warrior pose

The warrior pose has a number of benefits for children. On the physical side, it strengthens the shoulders and hips as flexibility and balance improve. Mentally, the Warrior pose improves concentration and helps children to feel empowered. Like the superhero pose, standing like a warrior can increase confidence. Have your child stand with their feet spread apart, turn one foot so that it is at a 90º angle to the other foot, leaning their weight on the foot they have turned. Ask them to raise their arms stretching their fingers in opposite directions. Then turn to face the direction of the bent knee. Repeat on the other side.

Cloud spotting

Ideally, you need a cloudy day with a decent breeze for this activity to work but when children concentrate on what they can see in the clouds, their focus is solely on the images rather than other things that may interrupt their thoughts. It is also an activity that encourages creativity and freedom to express their ideas because it's subjective, so there are no right or wrong answers!

Cosmic Kids

Cosmic Kids is a website with a YouTube channel that covers a number of skills for children. There are some popular stories that have been adapted to include yoga, mindfulness, and relaxation. It's a great way to engage children in activities that engage the body and the mind.

Balancing Act

This is similar to the Tree pose but adapted for children. Have children stand with their arms stretched to the sides and raise one leg. You may want to have a chair nearby in case they wobble. The idea of the activity is that they find a focal point in front of them and concentrate on that point for as long as possible. You can increase the intensity by adding distractions (like throwing a soft toy past them) and reminding them that the game is to block out these distractions.

Teddy bear breathing

I like this activity for younger children because it is sometimes hard for them to recognise the impact of their breathing and just how much control they have over it. Ask your little one to lay on the floor and place a teddy bear or other soft toy on their diaphragm (just below the rib cage and above the belly). First, start with normal breaths and have them watch how the bear moves. Gradually, have them increase the depth of their breaths to see how much more the bear moves.

Guided Imagery

Guided imagery is a type of relaxation and it's often a good starting place for meditation. The idea of a child emptying their thoughts and only focusing on their breathing might be too much considering how challenging it is for adults. Guided imagery literally provides a voice for children to listen to, taking them to a comfortable, happy, and safe place in order to calm their mind. You can use videos on guided imagery for children or you can guide them yourself.

Begin by having them get into a comfortable position and take a few deep breaths. Now, ask them to imagine a place that you go on to describe. This isn't the same as taking them to a happy place. With guided imagery, you want to describe a place that allows them to tap into their senses. For example, if you are talking about a beach, you wouldn't talk about the fun you have there. You would talk about the warmth they can feel on their face, the smell of the salt water, the feel of the sand between their fingers, and the sound of their waves.

Colour Mandalas

Mandalas have long been associated with mindfulness and inner calm. But colouring in general is a mindful exercise because it engages both hemispheres of the brain. To make colouring more mindful, ask your little one to think about the different colours, their tones, intensity, and what different colours look like next to each other. Ask them to think about how the pencil feels in their hand, a strange question that few people think about. Ask them if their mood changes when they choose different colours. These questions will help keep them focused on the present.

Finger Gratitude

As parents, I think any alternative to the Finger Family song is a welcome break and this finger-wiggling activity is another idea. Whether you choose to sing it or just talk about it, use your child's hands and each of the five fingers to talk about things they are grateful for. Again, give them some direction by holding up your hand, wiggling your thumb, and saying things like "I am grateful for all the hugs you give me.". If you want to explain why, this is a good extension of the activity.

1-minute meditation

Meditation is about removing all of the bustle in your mind and is often more difficult than mindfulness because mindfulness encourages focus to be on a particular object or sense. Meditation tends to rely focusing on breath work. The thought of doing this can be distressing for little people because of the time required. For this reason, try 1-minute meditation.

Sit down with your child and explain what is going to happen. Together, you are going to get comfortable and take 10 slow, deep breaths (this should take around 1 minute). In this minute, you aren't going to talk and if a thought pops into their head, that's ok, but they are going to let it float by and return back to their breathing. A timer may help. Afterward, talk about what they experienced in that minute. Adjust the amount of time if necessary. Remember that this isn't time for you to meditate but to be there to support your child. On the positive, this means you can take advantage of driving time and other situations where there is quiet.

COPING TIPS AND TRICKS FOR WARM TO HOT EMOTIONS

Many of the activities in this chapter are also coping strategies, so don't feel you have to rely only on the following. It's a good idea to experiment with the activities and create a list of 4 or 5 activities that your child really responds to. After all, each child is different and will prefer some activities over others. Here are a few more ideas you can try.

Communicating emotions to an adult

So far, most of our communication methods have involved your observation. As busy parents, you can't be watching them 24/7. And if you are busy, children also have to learn that they can't interrupt, despite how strong their feelings are. Try having a set of visual aids nearby. You can have a set of flashcards, they can choose the emotion they are feeling and if you are on the phone or dealing with siblings, they can come and put the flashcard next to you. Be sure to acknowledge you have seen the card and as soon as you are free, offer them support. You will be surprised, with practice, they may have resolved their problem before you get to them, they just wanted to tell you how they were feeling.

Ideas for self-soothing

As we learned from the polyvagal theory, the senses can be a wonderful way to help children self-soothe. Here are just some ideas that can engage your child's senses and comfort them at the same time.

- Sight: photos of friends, family or pets, their favourite book, images of nature, their favourite film or cartoon, or old pictures they have coloured.
- Hearing: Songs, musical toys, voice messages from friends, pre-recorded messages from you.
- Touch: Stroking their pet, a soft blanket or toy, sinking their hands in different textures like shaving foam, bubbly water, or slime.
- Taste: Have their favourite snacks handy, mix different flavours of juice, or allow them to choose their favourite meal for dinner.
- Smell: Encourage them to smell different herbs and spices as you cook, have scented lotions to choose from, or have them care for a special plant that smells nice.

The ice pack

Similar to cold water, the ice pack can have an instant calming effect because it stimulates the vagus nerve. Wrap some ice cubes, an ice pack, or just a bag of peas in a cloth. Have your little one hold it in their hands, lay down and place it on their chest, touch it to the back of their neck, the inside of their wrists, or the soles of their feet. Make sure they are moving it to different parts of their body to avoid prolonged contact and ice burn.

5-Minute energy burst

When emotions are really high, an energy burst is a great way to release built-up tension. It can be any number of activities such as running around the garden, skipping, hula hoop, jumping jacks, or turning up the music and dancing it out!

Emotional outlets

Some children may prefer less energetic ways to let go of built-up emotions. In these cases, it's great to encourage them to be creative and especially with messy play. You can get some shaving foam and add different food colourings for them to create 3D images, let them paint on paper or card, have some musical instruments to play, or if they are older, give them some prompts to create a story!

A coping box

Whether it's an old shoe box or something you save from a delivery, decorate your box and have your child fill it with things that make them happy. It could be a little figure they got, a special present, a photo, or even their favourite t-shirt. For extra comfort, you can give them a piece of your clothing that you have worn so that it smells of you.

Create a safe space

Somewhere in your home, carve out a little space that is just for them. It could be a corner or a play tent. You would be surprised how many children love sitting in a cupboard or a wardrobe. Stick happy images in the safe space, even consider adding a diffuser with their favourite scent, a blanket, and a torch for dark spaces. Let them know that this is a special place just for them when they need a break from their worries.

WHEN TO SEEK PROFESSIONAL HELP

The decision to seek professional help is often based on your instincts. Some indications that you might want to consider talking to a specialist include:

- Tantrums or meltdowns that last for hours
- Changes in routine and transitions are especially difficult for them
- They have difficulties and preschool or school
- They are easily distracted and distract you a lot
- Their moods are irregular, very much hot and cold with no in-between.

There are many types of professional help available but one that should be a high priority is play therapy. Play therapy looks like ordinary play time but a therapist puts themselves in the child's world and follows their lead while observing emotions and behaviour. Because children are more relaxed and open up during play, it makes it easier for the therapist to discover underlying issues. For example, a play therapist is able to analyse a drawing to discover if the child has relationship problems with a particular person. They will also understand how certain toys act as symbols for the child.

Play therapy can help with a wide range of problems from children who are facing chronic illnesses to aggressive behaviour, from developmental delays and disorders to traumatic experiences. Outcomes can include stronger relationships in school and at home, better coping strategies, increased empathy, and reduced anxiety, to name a few. If you are interested in more information, I highly recommend looking at the Play Therapy International website, or send me a message in our 'Kids Delayed Speech and Language Support Group on Facebook because we have a play therapist in the group.

One final note on when to seek professional help, and this is such a taboo subject because as parents, we are expected to just get on with it and cope. If you feel that you can't handle your child's emotions, even though it might not be affecting them to the same extent, it's okay to reach out for professional help. Parenting is challenging and there will be giant obstacles, but it shouldn't drain the life and soul out of you. Asking for help doesn't make you a bad parent!!

To end this chapter, I just want to take a moment to make sure we aren't reinforcing their emotional outbursts. This can be tricky because it's often things we have seen our own parents do and have picked up on habits. The biggest example is constantly trying to calm children down. The goal is to provide them with the techniques to do this themselves rather than you doing it all the time. As strange as this sounds, you also don't want to reward your child when they do calm down.

There is a big difference between emotions and behaviour. Children are allowed to experience the wide spectrum of emotions and manage each one. What they do as a result of that emotion is what should be praised or disciplined.

Let's say your child is feeling tense and instead of throwing toys around, they stand up and go to their safe place. As you would expect, in their safe place, they calm down. You need to praise the behaviour-going to the safe place. Children need attention but showering them with it may only reinforce the issue.

Our final chapter is a special one for me and not something that I normally include in books. However, because a positive role model is essential for emotional regulation in children, I have included a bonus chapter to help parents become more aware of their feelings and gain better control over them.

8

YOU HAVE GOT THIS: 13 ACTIVITIES JUST FOR PARENTS AND CAREGIVERS

Every activity, game, tip, and trick that we have covered will enable you to get better at handling your own emotions as well as your little one but let's face it, with a few more years on our shoulders, sometimes we need to take emotional regulation a step further and put it into context with our adult lives. This chapter is all about you so that you can excel and feel confident in your example setting, but more than this, you can really start to enjoy your role as a parent.

EMOTIONAL REGULATION SELF-ASSESSMENT

I'm not going to ask you to add up points and give you a final result. Instead, I would like you to consider the following statements and decide whether you strongly disagree,

disagree, agree, strongly agree, or if you feel neutral about it. The point is not to get a score, but to take a moment to self-reflect and discover your strengths and weaknesses.

1. I can label my emotions in different situations
2. I feel that my mood affects the people in my life
3. I find it easy to express my emotions
4. I find it easy to talk about my emotions
5. I feel I am good at recognising emotions in others
6. I know what to do when I start to overthink
7. When I am feeling down, I do something nice for myself
8. I take responsibility for my emotions
9. I am aware of my triggers
10. My family members understand and respect my limits
11. I give myself time when my emotions take over
12. I can accept that I am not perfect

Remember, there is no pass or fail here. Take a few moments to think about the answers, right them down if need be, and even go back later or another day in case other thoughts come to mind.

SELF-CARE

As a parent, the idea of self-care just sounds selfish but it is quite the contrary. Self-care is about making sure your physical and mental needs are met so that you are able to handle daily challenges. By making sure you exercise, eat well, get enough sleep, and take any medications you need to stay healthy, you will have the energy to deal with all of your responsibilities. Just like our children, emotional regulation is far harder when you are hungry, tired, or ill.

TAKE FIVE—RELIGIOUSLY!

At least once a day and most definitely every day, take 5 minutes just for you. It is only 5 minutes, so don't feel guilty. Step outside, stare out the window or savour your morning coffee. Teach yourself how to slow down and enjoy the calm. You don't have to meditate or be mindful, but it is a good idea to take in your surroundings and remind yourself that things aren't all bad.

TAKE A DIGITAL DETOX

There is no doubt that technology is essential in most of our lives, but we have taken this to the extent where we become a little obsessed. I got into the habit of taking 5 minutes for myself but then jumped on social media. One of two things happened. I was flooded with negativity and other people complaining or I lost track of time and felt guilty for not doing more important things. Both of these things led to feelings of anxiety, frustration, and anger and all of these emotions could have been avoided! Try to have half an hour each day that is technology-free.

REWIRING NEGATIVE THOUGHTS

We have thousands of negative thoughts on a daily basis and a large percentage of these are repetitive. Eventually, the cycle of negative thinking is going to leave you emotionally drained. You need to be able to recognise when a negative thought pops into your head and stop it before it spirals out of control. To do this, you need to begin by looking for evidence that supports your negative thought and then reframe it to make it realistic. Let's put that into practice.

- Negative thought: I'm a bad parent.
- The evidence: There is none. Your children have a roof over their heads, clothes on their backs, food in their tummies, and love in their hearts. On the contrary, you are a good parent because you are taking steps to become better.
- Reframing the negative thought: I'm not a perfect parent but I know I do my absolute best for my children.

Rewiring negative thoughts isn't about covering up the negative with a positive. It's about understanding if there is any truth behind how you feel. Because we live in quite a negative world and our brains tend to lean toward the negative, it's easy to believe the unhelpful and untrue things you tell yourself but with practice, you can reframe these thoughts and improve your self-esteem.

USING AFFIRMATIONS

Positive affirmations are another way to reduce the negative thoughts in your mind. I confess that I thought this was a little bit 'hippy' in the beginning but over the last couple of years, I admit I have noticed an improvement in my confidence.

The brain doesn't work in the past or in the future, so if you tell your brain a phrase in the present enough times, it starts to believe it is real. If it works for negative thoughts, the same theory can be applied to the positive! Think about one thing that you would like to change in your life and create a sentence about it, be sure to use I, make the sentence in the present tense, and avoid negative words like won't or don't. Here are some examples:

- I am proud of my mind and body
- I live life to the full
- I am confident and I am improving every day
- I am a good parent
- I trust my abilities and my strength

Some of you reading will have witnessed my issues on Facebook calls so you will understand that one of my affirmations is "I am a technology queen!".

HOW IS YOUR MINDSET?

Remember when you were younger and you had all these ambitions? Do you ever feel like after the house and the children, your own dreams and goals seemed to be put to one side or forgotten? As an adult with healthy emotions, you need to get back your growth mindset. When the children are fast asleep, ignore the pile of ironing, put on your favourite music, and grab a pen and paper. Write a list of fresh goals for the short-term and the long-term. These are your goals so don't include goals for the family. Maybe you want to start a business, maybe you want to learn how to restore furniture, or take up a new hobby. Break these goals down into different steps and decide what needs to be done to achieve the first step.

STOPP

STOPP is an acronym for Stop, Take a breath, Observe, Put things in perspective, and Practice. It encourages you to pause before acting, to be mindful of your breathing, to look at the situation as a whole, and then look at it from different perspectives. Finally, you can act based on the based possible outcome rather than your initial emotion.

HOW BIG ARE YOUR PROBLEMS?

At some point, we are all guilty of making mountains out of molehills. Say you forgot to put a piece of fruit in your child's packed lunch and all of a sudden, you are the world's worst parent. It's a good idea to take a few minutes to analyse problems and put them on a scale of 1 to 5 to decipher just how serious it is.

- Level One: Minor hiccup- you are running a bit late, you didn't quite finish the dishes before leaving home, your child is wearing odd socks- again!
- Level Two: Small issue- you didn't check that your child finished their homework, you have no idea what to cook for dinner, children aren't listening.
- Level Three: It's a problem but short-term- you aren't feeling great, your child has a minor accident, you are dreading something at work.
- Level Four: It's causing a lack of sleep- financial worries, you had a fight with someone, a parent becomes more dependent on you.
- Level Five: It's an emergency- a natural disaster, serious danger, it's life-threatening.

Problems in levels 1 to 3, on the greater scale of things, aren't really problems. Level 4 is going to require extra time and energy but it's only really level 5 problems that should be a cause for our extremely intense feelings.

REASSESS THE PEOPLE IN YOUR LIFE

This is a difficult one but crucial for your emotions. Over the years, we make friends and some stick with us, and others move on. Out of those that stick around, you may find there are one or two that rub you up the wrong way. Perhaps they overstep boundaries, they are constantly negative or draining you of your energy. It might even be the case that they manipulate you or only use you when they need something from you. It's hard to break ties with these people but consider whether they are doing more harm than good. This can be true for some family members too. If you can't completely remove them from your life, at least create some extra distance so they can't impact your emotions to the same extent.

UNDERSTAND THE POWER OF CHOICE

You may have noticed that I am a bit of a fan of quotes and here is my final quote for you. These words of wisdom come from Viktor Frankl, a Holocaust survivor who lost both his parents in concentration camps.

> *"Between stimulus and response there is a space. In that space is our power to choose our response. In our response lies our growth and freedom."*

This space Frankl talks of may only be a split second but it is always there. You have the ability to choose how you respond to your emotions and how you respond to other people's emotions. On a larger scale, you have the power to choose no over always saying yes to someone. Rather than feeling like you have little control over your life, look at the things that you can control.

STEP BACK FROM PERFECTIONISM

This is another thing that I have had to learn from experience but expecting yourself and even others around you to be perfect only leads to disappointment, frustration, and anxiety, if not worse. We all like to have a clean and tidy home but the truth is, you can spend 2 hours cleaning and if you are lucky, it will stay that way for 30 minutes. And this is only one example in life. Nothing will ever be 100 per cent perfect and that's okay. That is what keeps us striving for more, it keeps us learning and motivated. As soon as you stop expecting things to be perfect, you can protect yourself from feeling like you are a failure. Reward your efforts, not the outcome. After doing the housework, I look around and tell myself that it's not perfect, but it's certainly better than it was!

HAVE FUN

Finally, something that we rarely make an effort to do because our focus is making sure little people are happy and laughing, do something that is fun for you. I want all of the activities to be fun for your children and also for you but that still isn't quite the same as having some adult fun. And again, it can be just a case of finding those 5 minutes a day to do something that puts a smile on your face or even better, a full-on belly-giggle. Dance, explore, plan a party, try a new recipe, or do an activity that you used to do as a child. Your child needs to see you happy but more than that, you deserve it!

Finally, learn how to forgive yourself for the mistakes you make. Sometimes, life will get the better of you and you will snap. Needless to say, you will look at your little one's shocked face and feel terrible, then you will likely try to overcompensate for your outburst before going to bed and replaying it in your mind. None of these actions are productive. Accept everyone makes mistakes at some point but be that shining example once again. Own your mistake, apologise, and keep moving forward.

CONCLUSION

Our emotions are incredibly complex. They aren't clean and clearly defined. You don't just have a feeling and move on from it. It's more like that one red sock you put in with a load of white washing. Mixed, messy, and require more attention than you realised! Few adults are fortunate to have grown up in a home where emotional awareness and regulation were a priority, so this leaves us in a situation where we don't always practice what we preach.

From the moment children are born, they are taking in the world around them and absorbing all the emotions they witness. They learn to copy, express how they feel, and understand how you feel even before they first words. As they reach certain ages, their range of emotions begins to increase, yet they still don't have the ability to express them all in the right way. It's a learning curve!

Just as you are there to teach them how to take their first steps or how to colour between the lines, you can be there to support them with this essential life skill. Children who learn how to label their feelings and how to cope with the bigger emotions will grow up to have fewer issues with their social skills, they will develop stronger and healthier relationships, they can have better academic outcomes, and even though this is years away, they will become happier and more successful adults.

Though the final chapter was to help with your own emotional regulation, this is the first place for you to start. It's not easy but you will appreciate that this is a skill that takes time and work, not just something that you can read and master straight away. When you appreciate this, you will have greater empathy for your child who is also learning as they go through different struggles.

I mentioned getting down to your child's level when playing and talking to them in order to make them feel more comfortable and make better eye contact but there is another reason to do this. When you look at the world from a child's point of view, you can see that things are a little scarier than you thought. Their older sibling is short in comparison to you, but they are a giant compared to them.

Your child has problems that may not seem like a problem to you, but to them, it's the only thing on their mind at that moment and it's frustrating. When you can't get the lid off a jar, you can almost become obsessed with the challenge, using a tea towel, tapping it with a knife, and banging it against the side. You get frustrated. Now imagine a child trying to force a puzzle piece where it's not supposed to go. You can see the solution and struggle to comprehend why they throw themselves into a fit of rage. They can't!

As you begin to label your emotions more accurately, your children will follow suit. If they have witnessed you stubbornly shouting at that jam jar lid and then say "Sorry, I became a little bit frustrated then", they will copy you and label their emotions as they arise. To get better at labelling so many different emotions, you don't need a degree in child psychology. You simply need to play games and do activities that are focused on emotional awareness.

It's handy to have an "emotional kit" so that you are prepared for the different activities. Have a box with paints and a ton of magazine clippings with images of different facial expressions. Save old socks to make puppets and anything else that can be recycled into a game. It's a good idea to have a pot of bubbles and a bag of balloons in there too, just because these are very versatile items.

As much as we want to jump in, helping children handle their emotions is very much an observational task. Observe them while they play, and let them lead the play rather than you telling them what certain puppets or toys should be doing. Watch them as they are out and about or playing with other children. Above all, don't forget to listen to them! Ask questions, empathise, and validate their feelings instead of telling them that they shouldn't feel a certain way. Talk about how you feel and what you do when you have feelings that can lead to negative behaviour. Be the support, be available, and be the safety and comfort that they need, but don't do it all for them. Children need opportunities to practice emotional regulation and they need to feel that they are safe to do so.

Although emotions are complex, teaching emotional regulation doesn't have to be. You know have 103 activities to get you started. Some of which you can do straight away, with no effort or materials. My final piece of advice would be to keep a journal of your experiences. This will help you keep track of your little one's progress and also give you an additional outlet for your feelings.

If you need some extra help with things like potty training, speech and language development, or making progress, remember to click on the link in the beginning of the book so more support. If you can think of something that isn't covered in my books, drop me a message!

I always love to hear about how parents get on and a short Amazon review is a great way to let me know what games you have tried and the fun you both had. Amazon reviews are also crucial because you aren't the only caregivers who might be struggling with how to help their children. Sharing your opinions lets other parents know that there are plenty of things they can be doing to support their children with their emotions. It would be great if you could take a few seconds to help these parents too.

Good luck and have lots of fun playing!

You can scan the QR code or visit the link below to leave a quick review!

https://www.amazon.co.uk/dp/B0BZRXB3PX?geniuslink=true

REFERENCES

American Psychological Association. (2019, December 12). *Students do better in school when they can understand, manage emotions: Emotionally intelligent students get better grades and higher test scores, study says.* ScienceDaily. https://www.sciencedaily.com/releases/2019/12/191212095906.htm

Firestone, L., PhD. (2019, December 13). *Why we need to teach kids emotional intelligence.* Psychology Today. https://www.psychologytoday.com/us/blog/compassion-matters/201603/why-we-need-teach-kids-emotional-intelligence

Hunziker, U. A., & Barr, R. G. (1986, May). *Increased carrying reduces infant crying: A randomised controlled trial.* NIH. https://pubmed.ncbi.nlm.nih.gov/3517799/

Kreiss, T. (2014, October 27). *The creativity post | power-posing like a superhero transforms you. . ..* The Creativity Post. https://www.creativitypost.com/article/power_posing_like_a_super_hero_transforms_you_into_one

Martín-Requejo, K., & Santiago-Ramajo, S. (2021, September 3). *Reduced emotional intelligence in children aged 9-11 caused by the COVID-19 pandemic London.* NIH. https://www.ncbi.nlm.nih.gov/pmc/articles/PMC8661734/

Marusak, H. A. (2022, September 8). *Meditation holds the potential to help treat children suffering from traumas, difficult diagnoses or other stressors – a behavioural neuroscientist explains.* The Conversation. https://theconversation.com/meditation-holds-the-potential-to-help-treat-children-suffering-from-traumas-difficult-diagnoses-or-other-stressors-a-behavioural-neuroscientist-explains-189037

Mcleod, S. (2014). *Bobo Doll Experiment - Simply Psychology.* https://www.simplypsychology.org/bobo-doll.html

My Mood My Choices. (2019, May 21). *7 Steps to Increase Your Child's EQ.* My Moods, My Choices. https://mymoodsmychoices.com/blogs/news/7-steps-to-increase-your-childs-eq

Printed in Great Britain
by Amazon